Poverty *vs* Wealth

Poverty *vs* Wealth

FUNDAMENTALS OF PROSPERITY

First Edition

Roger Braker

http://PovertyvsWealth.com
http://FundamentalsofProsperity.com

This book it presented for your consideration only and we make no warranties, written or implied as to its accuracy or completeness.

Thanks to all the people that helped me to understand this subject by your books, CDs and thanks to God for opening my eyes. Without that there is no true understanding.

Contents

Poverty vs. Wealth: An Introduction to Fundamentals of Prosperity

There are two things in life that seem to distract people quite a bit: sex and money. Fortunately, both are covered in the Bible. In 1 Corinthians 7 God, by revelation, lays out some good instructions regarding sexual relations for people in the church, so that, as it says in **1 Corinthians 7:35,** "that ye may attend upon the Lord without distraction."

Money and finances are also a great distraction for many people. If you are broke all the time or in poverty, that can be a huge distraction. Generally, the distraction is lack of funds to pay current bills. The purpose of this book is to show the proper foundational truths, from the Bible, about how to handle finances from the Bible. Then you can learn to incorporate those truths into your life. As you incorporate them, the distraction over finances should cease because you will cease to be broke or in poverty. How to deal with money has been much goobered up by religion over the centuries and it is not conveniently covered in one chapter as sex has been in 1 Corinthians. But as we read we can see the plan that God has laid out for us so that we are not distracted by finances either. Then we can "attend upon the Lord without distraction" in that part of our life also.

Forward

The principles in this book took us years to learn, so have some patience with yourself if you are just starting. Start in on the book, and as you see things that make sense put them into practice in your life. Then reread the book and as you find more ideas that make sense, incorporate them as well. If you put the principles of God's Word into action, He will teach you if you want to know.

Here is a list of questions that we are going to attempt to answer as well as some cloudy areas that we will take a look at when it comes to money.

1. Are tithing and giving the same?
2. Is it easier for God to prosper self-employed people than salaried ones?
3. If someone were to give you $10,000.00, write down what you would do with it.
4. Does God expect us to save anything for the future?
5. Why do some give and give, and yet prosperity seems to escape them?
6. What are the differences between promises and warnings?
7. Why are the warnings about money better known than the promises of prosperity?
8. How do you "live within your means?"
9. What if you lost it all?

There are invisible laws that make up the universe that we live in. There are laws of mathematics, chemistry, physics, gravity, airlift, and also laws that cover the handling of money. You cannot touch, taste, feel, see or hear them but they work none the less. The laws of money work the same way every time just as the laws of mathematics do.

We are not going to cover where to invest your money or what kind of markets to be in. We also are not going to cover making money, but we **are** interested in the fundamentals of prosperity, on handling the money that we do have. The fundamentals of prosperity have nothing to do with what kind of job we have, who we work for, or who our parents are.

Many people look for prosperity in books and seminars. They try flipping real estate, reading positive thinking books, and try reading how the rich think. They start at the wrong end of the subject. Even if they end up making a large amount, they may easily lose it all because of a lack of the fundamentals. These fundamentals of prosperity are essential to a prosperous life. **Without** an understanding of these fundamentals of prosperity, you could have a pro sports contract, inherit the money, win the lottery, or find gold coins buried in a milk can, but you may end up losing it all and living in poverty with no hope of ever regaining it. **With** an understanding of the fundamentals of prosperity, you can become very prosperous without a pro sports contract and have a good chance of keeping it.

(All emphasis indicated by bold typeface or underlining in scripture verses was added by the author of this book and, unless otherwise noted, all scripture is from the Kings James Version)

**_(All emphasized, bold type or underlined, are to be read with great emphasis.
The bold is because that is crux of the statement or the reason the verse is being read.)_**

Poverty *vs* Wealth

Wish Above All Things

I am not a prosperity teacher or minister. The rules or principles of prosperity should be as much a part of our lives as many other parts of walking with and for God are. This is just one topic, and it is the topic of this book.

Two of the greatest areas of concern in life are wealth and health. As we age these become even more important. In light of this, the Epistle of III John has a very interesting verse.

> **3 John 1:2** Beloved, I wish above all things that thou mayest prosper and be in health, even as thy soul prospereth.

Think about this: it is nothing for us to talk after fellowship or church about things that affect our health and nutrition and then to study nutrition during the week. But the subject of finances has been stigmatized for hundreds of years to the end that most Christians don't speak much about it.

Our adversary, the devil, has attacked the subject of health, to the end that many Christians believe it is God's will for them to be sick. This enemy also, through devilish doctrines, has caused many Christians to believe that if you have much money you must have gotten it through shady means, and that you are greedy. The devil has put forth that the most humble people are poor.

A good friend of mine, Rev. Mike Verdicchio, wrote a book and produced a CD on healing that are very good. The book shows that it is God's will for you to be whole - that by the stripes of Jesus Christ you were healed. Links to these are provided in the back of this book.

Some people feel that prosperity and health are inextricably interwoven:
> Great wealth but bed ridden?
> Great health but in poverty?

God wants us to have both together. Great health AND prosperity. These are two of the biggest areas of concern in many people's lives. It is the desire of God that we are all prosperous and healthy.

If both health and prosperity are part of God's will, then **both** should be acceptable to study.

Christianity has taught that if you speak of money then you are greedy. If to desire great health is to desire God's will for your life, then to desire great prosperity should be just as acceptable as part of God's will for your life. A steady diet of teaching from God's Word, listened to every day, could prosper your soul, increase your believing, and increase your understanding of God's Word.

Could that, then, have an impact on your prosperity and health? **Change your life?**

This subject of prosperity should be part of our life as much as any other part of walking with and for God is. My goal is to help get to the root of what God promises about prosperity and then believe that.

As you look at this information and find things you can use, think on this:

> **Psalm 119:97-100** MEM. O how love I thy law! it *is* my meditation all the day. Thou through thy commandments hast made

me wiser than mine enemies: for they *are* ever with me. I have more understanding than all my teachers: for thy testimonies *are* my meditation. I understand more than the ancients, because I keep thy precepts.

Notice that the Psalmist says he meditated on God's Word all the day. Because he did that, God gave him wisdom above all his enemies. **And** that as he meditated on the scriptures, he had more understanding than all his teachers. Last of all, he says that because he **kept** God's precepts or God's Word, he had more understanding than the ancients. WOW!

As you read and think and read and think, ask God to teach you. He will. Your understanding will grow and grow. As you put His Word into action, He will teach you even more. Understanding is a growing process. You may not get it all the first day or even the first year. Being faithful to thinking on His Word and incorporating it into your life will bring great understanding and will be of great profit to you and the family, and the house that you are building.

Proverbs 14:1 Every wise woman buildeth her house: but the foolish plucketh it down with her hands.

Chapter 1

What Comes First?

My motivation in writing this is to learn and to believe what God has promised. Then we can believe what He has said, carry it out, and then see His Word come to pass in our lives.

We are not after money in this book so much as we are after a greater relationship with our Father. We want to know what He has said and promised to us as His children. To paraphrase another man, "It is not what you get; it is what you become in the process." In this case it would be a deeper or greater walk with our Father with far fewer distractions as we learn about this field of prosperity.

To reiterate, my motivation for learning this subject was to find out what God actually said and then build my believing of prosperity on those words.

So let's get started:

> **3 John 1:2** Beloved, I wish above all things that thou mayest prosper and be in health, even as thy soul prospereth.

God's desire for us as He states in His Word is that we prosper and be in health, even as our soul prospers. With both health and prosperity, there are promises and principles in God's Word concerning how to obtain both. For instance, with health, we have the truth that "by his stripes we were healed," and we have the principle that "a merry heart does us good like a medicine". The first part here is a promise, and the second part is a way we can learn to conduct our lives to manifest health by having a merry or happy heart.

So it is with prosperity. We are going to start with the principle of keeping God first and see some of what that may mean. Along the way, we will see some principles that go along with the promises. Here in Matthew, it states:

> **Matthew 6:31-33** Therefore take no thought, saying, What shall we eat? or, What shall we drink? or, Wherewithal shall we be clothed? (For after all these things do the Gentiles seek:) for your heavenly Father knoweth that ye have need of all these things. But seek ye first the kingdom of God, and his righteousness; and all these things shall be added unto you.

We learn that if we keep God first and seek Him, He will add the things we need to our lives. If we seek after the things, we may never find them or never be satisfied with what we have.

Jesus Christ spoke about one of the first problems we run into when it comes to prosperity and wealth.

> **Matthew 6:24** No man can serve two masters: for either he will hate the one, and love the other; or else he will hold to the one, and despise the other. Ye cannot serve God and mammon.

"Hate" is the antithesis of love, as it is active ill will; "hold" is to cling to the one; "despise" is to think less upon or think down upon. We cannot serve God and mammon (the world or things in the world).

The Weymouth New Testament:

> **Matthew 6:24** "No man can be the bondservant of two masters; for either he will dislike one and like the other, or he will attach

himself to one and think slightingly of the other. You cannot be the bondservants both of God and of gold.

If you try to serve, love or trust in both, you would be double minded, and James speaks on that:

James 1:8 A double minded man is unstable in all his ways.

So when we endeavor to serve both, we are double minded and therefore unstable.

The truth of keeping God first is stated in Matthew 6:33, but to see examples of people who did that, we can look in the Old Testament which was written for our learning. Many times the New Testament gives us the finely stated truths, but to see examples of those truths we need to look in the Old Testament.

> **Romans 15:4** For whatsoever things were written aforetime were written for **our** learning, that we through patience and comfort of the scriptures might have hope.

Consider Hezekiah:

> **2 Chronicles 29:1-5** Hezekiah began to reign *when he was* five and twenty years old, and he reigned nine and twenty years in Jerusalem. And his mother's name *was* Abijah, the daughter of Zechariah. And he did *that which was* right in the sight of the LORD, according to all that David his father had done. He in the first year of his reign, in the first month, opened the doors of the house of the LORD, and repaired them. And he brought in the priests and the Levites, and gathered them together into the east street, And said unto them, Hear me, ye Levites, sanctify now yourselves, and sanctify the house of the LORD God of your fathers, and carry forth the filthiness out of the holy *place*.

This is the very first thing Hezekiah did -- he cleaned out the

Temple and repaired it. Then he held a Passover in the second month. It was supposed to be held in the first month, but they could not do it then because the Temple was not cleaned out. The Law allowed the Passover to be kept in the second month in some cases, so this was legal.

> **2 Chronicles 30:1, 2** And Hezekiah sent to all Israel and Judah, and wrote letters also to Ephraim and Manasseh, that they should come to the house of the LORD at Jerusalem, to keep the passover unto the LORD God of Israel. For the king had taken counsel, and his princes, and all the congregation in Jerusalem, to keep the passover in the second month.

God showed us what Hezekiah kept first in his heart; he honored God first in the establishment of his reign. Now in the records of Hezekiah, we see God's prospering of Hezekiah and God's deliverance from Judah's enemies.

> **2 Kings 18:5-7** He trusted in the LORD God of Israel; so that after him was none like him among all the kings of Judah, nor *any* that were before him. For he clave to the LORD, *and* departed not from following him, but kept his commandments, which the LORD commanded Moses. And the LORD was with him; *and* he prospered whithersoever he went forth: and he rebelled against the king of Assyria, and served him not.

In the first Psalm, the Psalmist explains some of how keeping God first works:

> **Psalm 1:1-3** Blessed *is* the man that walketh not in the counsel of the ungodly, nor standeth in the way of sinners, nor sitteth in the seat of the scornful. But his delight *is* in the law of the LORD; and in his law doth he meditate day and night. And he shall be like a tree planted by the rivers of water, that bringeth forth his fruit in his season; his leaf also shall not wither; and whatsoever he doeth shall prosper.

The Psalmist delighted and meditated in God's Word. God's Word came first in the Psalmist's life.Because he kept God and His Word first in his heart, the Psalmist brought forth fruit at the right time in his life, and he prospered wherever he went.

With Hezekiah you see that God was first in his heart because his first action as king was to clean out the temple, to reestablish the worship of God, and then to keep the Passover. As you read about his reign, you then see God prospering him and delivering him.

Here is another example. This record took place just after Judah was carried away into the Babylonian captivity.

> **Daniel 1:1-8** In the third year of the reign of Jehoiakim king of Judah came Nebuchadnezzar king of Babylon unto Jerusalem, and besieged it. And the Lord gave Jehoiakim king of Judah into his hand, with part of the vessels of the house of God: which he carried into the land of Shinar to the house of his god; and he brought the vessels into the treasure house of his god. And the king spake unto Ashpenaz the master of his eunuchs, that he should bring *certain* of the children of Israel, and of the king's seed, and of the princes; Children in whom *was* no blemish, but well favoured, and skilful in all wisdom, and cunning in knowledge, and understanding science, and such as *had* ability in them to stand in the king's palace, and whom they might teach the learning and the tongue of the Chaldeans. And the king appointed them a daily provision of the king's meat, and of the wine which he drank: so nourishing them three years, that at the end thereof they might stand before the king.   Now among these were of the children of Judah, Daniel, Hananiah, Mishael, and Azariah: Unto whom the prince of the eunuchs gave names: for he gave unto Daniel *the name* of Belteshazzar; and to Hananiah, of Shadrach; and to Mishael, of Meshach; and to Azariah, of Abednego. But Daniel purposed in his heart that he would not defile himself with the portion of the king's meat, nor with the wine which

he drank: therefore he requested of the prince of the eunuchs that he might not defile himself.

It was against the Old Testament Law to eat the meat or to drink the wine that had been offered to idols. These would have been offered in the temples to the gods and then brought to the king's palace for consumption. This is what would have been served to these men. Daniel and the other three in the record had determined to keep God first no matter what. God then honored these men with great positions of power and influence in the kingdom of Babylon.

There are other records like this, but these two examples are of men that kept God first, and then God prospered them.

Keeping God first not only pays great rewards now but at the time rewards are given at the gathering together as well. We will see that in a minute.

These men loved God, honored Him, and trusted Him above all else. These men had great respect for God and His Word, and that is why when it was their time to stand on God's Word, God came first. God coming first was simply a manifestation of what they had put in their hearts a long time before. Notice that the inward part comes first; then what is produced in their lives is simply a manifestation of what they had already put in their hearts.

The following record is about a man that trusted in his wealth more than he loved God.

> **Mark 10:17-31** And when he was gone forth into the way, there came one running, and kneeled to him, and asked him, Good Master, what shall I do that I may inherit eternal life? And Jesus said unto him, Why callest thou me good? *there is* none good but one, *that is,* God. Thou knowest the commandments, Do not commit adultery, Do not kill, Do not steal, Do not bear false witness, Defraud not, Honour thy father and mother. And he

answered and said unto him, Master, all these have I observed
from my youth. Then Jesus beholding him loved him, and said
unto him, One thing thou lackest: go thy way, sell whatsoever
thou hast, and give to the poor, and thou shalt have treasure
in heaven: and come, take up the cross, and follow me. And he
was sad at that saying, and went away grieved: for he had great
possessions. And Jesus looked round about, and saith unto his
disciples, How hardly shall they that have riches enter into the
kingdom of God! And the disciples were astonished at his words.
But Jesus answereth again, and saith unto them, Children, how
hard is it for them that **trust in riches** to enter into the kingdom
of God! It is easier for a camel to go through the eye of a needle,
than for a rich man to enter into the kingdom of God. And they
were astonished out of measure, saying among themselves, Who
then can be saved? And Jesus looking upon them saith, With
men *it is* impossible, but not with God: for with God all things
are possible. Then Peter began to say unto him, Lo, we have left
all, and have followed thee. And Jesus answered and said, Verily I
say unto you, There is no man that hath left house, or brethren, or
sisters, or father, or mother, or wife, or children, or lands, for my
sake, and the gospel's, But he shall receive an hundredfold now
in this time, houses, and brethren, and sisters, and mothers, and
children, and lands, with persecutions; and in the world to come
eternal life. But many *that are* first shall be last; and the last first.

Notice that the man's problem **was not that he was rich**, but that
he **trusted** in those riches. His possessions and prosperity, not God,
came first in his life. He served the world, trusted in riches, and loved
his money more than he loved God. This is always a problem.

Also note that if he had been willing to give it all away and put God
first, God would have given it all back one hundred fold. So the issue
was not just that he was wealthy, but that he **trusted in his wealth**.

(An interesting note here: Abraham was very wealthy as was
Job and many others, but they did not have the problem this

man had. They trusted, loved and kept God first, not their possessions. So when it says Jesus loved him, he saw what the man's problem was and offered him the solution. If the man had heeded it, God would have given it all back and much more. Abraham did not need to do that, neither did Job or many others. This was just for that man. It is a lesson not to trust in anything other than God. It is a lesson to **keep Him first**. Then you do not need to do as this man needed to do.)

Psalm 35:27 Let them shout for joy, and be glad, that favour my righteous cause: yea, let them say continually, Let the LORD be magnified, <u>**which hath pleasure in the prosperity of his servant.**</u>

As long as we keep God first in our hearts, love Him and trust Him, He will add to us all that we need. What we need is what God has promised in His Word and what He will do for those that put their trust in Him.

Here is another record of a man who asked Jesus a question:

Luke 12:13-15 And one of the company said unto him, Master, speak to my brother, that he divide the inheritance with me. And he said unto him, Man, who made me a judge or a divider over you? And he said unto them, Take heed, and beware of covetousness: for a man's life consisteth not in the abundance of the things which he possesseth.

Hebrews 13:5 *Let your* conversation *be* without covetousness; *and be* content with such things as ye have: for he hath said, I will never leave thee, nor forsake thee.

We have no need to be envious of what others have even if we actually should have had part of it, such as an inheritance. Why? God has promised to supply our needs and fill our homes with His treasures, as we shall see, so that we have no need of going to the law to force others to give us something.

Keeping God first is the first and greatest of the fundamental principles of prosperity that we are going to consider. Practicing these principles of prosperity should be such a part of our lives that we barely think about it. Then we can spend our days keeping God first and prospering in this life He has given us.

Chapter 2

What is Prosperity?

3 John 1:2 Beloved, I wish above all things that thou mayest prosper and be in health, even as thy soul prospereth.

What really is prosperity? In <u>A Journey through Acts and Epistles, Volume 2</u>, the footnote on this verse says: "prosper: to be led in a good way or on a good path, to have a prosperous journey, to be well guided, to be successful.... Success in all matters would include material needs, health, peace of mind, joy in fellowship and other matters."

In this book we are mainly interested in the area of material needs.

Dictionary.com defines prosperity as:
1. a successful, flourishing, or thriving condition, especially in financial respects; good fortune.
2. prosperities, prosperous circumstances, characterized by financial success or good fortune.

Many see prosperity on a very short term basis -- a raise at work, or an unexpected check in the mail, or a good deal on a car, or to catch the right sale at the supermarket. These things are wonderful but not what actually results in long term prosperity.

The Art of Manliness website had a great explanation of prosperity in its article, "The Paycheck Mentality vs. the Net Worth Mentality":

"From the time we are old enough to understand, society conditions us to confuse income with wealth. We believe that doctors, CEOs, professional athletes, and movie actors are rich because they earn high incomes. We judge the economic success of our friends, relatives, and colleagues at work by how much money they earn. Six and seven- figure salaries are regarded as status symbols of wealth. Although there is a definite relationship between income and wealth, they are very separate and distinct economic measures. Income is how much money you earn in a given period of time. If you earn a million in a year and spend it all, you add nothing to your wealth. You're just living lavishly. Those who focus only on net income as a measure of economic success are ignoring the most important measuring stick of financial independence. **It's not how much you make, it's how much you keep.**"

http://www.artofmanliness.com/2015/02/16/net-worth-mentality/

The whole article is well worth reading.

Some people that make lists say there are over 2,000 verses on financial prosperity in the Bible. It must be an important topic, yet how many of them do we know?

Now, these promises of prosperity are to those who seek after God—very important to remember.

> **Deuteronomy 8:18** But thou shalt remember the LORD thy God: for *it is* he that giveth thee power to get wealth, that he may establish his covenant which he sware unto thy fathers, as *it is* this day.

> **Deuteronomy 28:2-8** And all these blessings shall come on thee, and overtake thee, if thou shalt hearken unto the voice of the LORD thy God. Blessed *shalt* thou *be* in the city, and blessed *shalt* thou *be* in the field. Blessed *shall be* the fruit of thy body, and the fruit of thy ground, and the fruit of thy cattle,

the increase of thy kine, and the flocks of thy sheep. Blessed *shall be* thy basket and thy store. Blessed *shalt* thou *be* when thou comest in, and blessed *shalt* thou *be* when thou goest out. The LORD shall cause thine enemies that rise up against thee to be smitten before thy face: they shall come out against thee one way, and flee before thee seven ways. The LORD shall command the blessing upon thee in thy storehouses, and in all that thou settest thine hand unto; and he shall bless thee in the land which the LORD thy God giveth thee.

Leviticus 25:19-22 And the land shall yield her fruit, and ye shall eat your fill, and dwell therein in safety. And if ye shall say, What shall we eat the seventh year? Behold, we shall not sow, nor gather in our increase: Then I will command my blessing upon you in the sixth year, and it shall bring forth fruit for three years. And ye shall sow the eighth year, and eat *yet* of old fruit until the ninth year; until her fruits come in ye shall eat *of* the old *store.*

"Command the Blessing upon" is a rare phrase and is used here with prosperity.

Deuteronomy 28:11-13 And the LORD shall make thee plenteous in goods, in the fruit of thy body, and in the fruit of thy cattle, and in the fruit of thy ground, in the land which the LORD sware unto thy fathers to give thee. The LORD shall open unto thee his good treasure, the heaven to give the rain unto thy land in his season, and to bless all the work of thine hand: and thou shalt lend unto many nations, and thou shalt not borrow. And the LORD shall make thee the head, and not the tail; and thou shalt be above only, and thou shalt not be beneath; if that thou hearken unto the commandments of the LORD thy God, which I command thee this day, to observe and to do *them:*

God will open to you His good treasure. God has many things stored up in abundance for His children. We have been told for many years that if we use too much, we will run out of land, water, oil, and all natural resources. But it is not true. We should not be wasteful, but God is not up all night working to create more trees because we are running out of them. He has great storehouses or treasuries to draw from.

God promises us prosperity, and that is only natural as we are His offspring, His children. Why would our Father who owns the earth and the fullness thereof want His children to live in poverty? He doesn't!!

> **Jeremiah 17:7-8** Blessed *is* the man that trusteth in the LORD, and whose hope the LORD is. For he shall be as a tree planted by the waters, and *that* spreadeth out her roots by the river, and shall not see when heat cometh, but her leaf shall be green; and shall not be careful in the year of drought, neither shall cease from yielding fruit.

So these promises we are looking at are for those that trust in and that seek after God and His promises.

Part of all you earn is yours to keep. -- *The Richest Man in Babylon*

(This book was originally written as a series of pamphlets around the early 1900s. Bankers had them written to encourage people to save their money. The pamphlets were eventually combined into a book)

CHAPTER 3

Filthy Lucre

While my wife and I were watching TV the other night and visiting about this book, a commercial came on advertising a TV show called: BLOOD AND OIL. The tag line at the end of the commercial was: **"Sometimes you have to play dirty to get filthy rich."**

To get a better understanding of prosperity from the Bible's point of view, we need to look at where this idea of filthy rich or the idea of money being filthy came from.

The term "filthy lucre" means: greed for wealth or material gain.

Lucre
Oxford Dictionary:

Money, especially when regarded as sordid or distasteful or gained in a dishonorable way. "officials getting their hands grubby with **filthy lucre**"
(http://www.oxforddictionaries.com/us/definition/american_english/lucre)

Filthy rich
Very rich, possibly having become so by unfair means. This little phrase can't be explained without looking at the word lucre. From the 14th century lucre has meant money and is referred

to as such by no less writers than Chaucer and John Wycliffe. These references generally included a negative connotation and gave rise to the terms "foul lucre" and "filthy lucre", which have been in use since the 16th century. "Filthy lucre" appears first in print in 1526 in the works of William Tyndale: "Teaching things which they ought not, because of filthy lucre." Here, Tyndale was using the term to mean dishonorable gain.

Following on the term "filthy lucre", money became known by the slang term "the filthy", and it isn't a great leap from there to the rich being called the "filthy rich". This was first used as a noun phrase meaning "rich people; who have become so by dishonorable means".

(http://www.phrases.org.uk/meanings/filthy-rich.html)

The pairing of filthy and lucre was meant, of course, to highlight the sinfulness of immoderate, greedy or shameful desire for wealth, and this was soon applied to the money itself and then onto the people that had a lot of money. How much is a lot of money? Generally, it is just more than what **you** have!!!

You can also see how the idea that if you have very much money, you must have had some greed in your life and gained it through dishonest or shameful dealings. Therefore, you have been tainted as well as the money. In some churches the wealthy feel shunned or closed off because others think that the wealthy must have gained their money through dishonesty. While discussing this book in my chiropractor's office he volunteered the information that his family, that is made up of doctors and lawyers who are very well off, are avoided by most people in their church because the people feel that the family is too well off.

The idea of having much money being sinful started as early as 100 AD and came into its own around 300 AD. Here are some quotes from the early Church Fathers:

You are not making a gift of your possession to the poor person.
You are handing over to him what is his.
Ambrose of Milan, 340-397.

The property of the wealthy holds them in chains . . . which
shackle their courage and choke their faith and hamper their
judgment and throttle their souls. They think of themselves as
owners, whereas it is they rather who are owned: enslaved as
they are to their own property, they are not the masters of their
money but its slaves.
Cyprian, 300 A.D.

The bread in your cupboard belongs to the hungry man; the
coat hanging in your closet belongs to the man who needs it;
the shoes rotting in your closet belong to the man who has
no shoes; the money which you put into the bank belongs to
the poor. You do wrong to everyone you could help but fail
to help.
Basil of Caesarea, 330-370 A.D.

Not to enable the poor to share in our goods is to steal from
them and deprive them of life. The goods we possess are not
ours but theirs.
John Chrysostom, 347-407 AD

Instead of the tithes which the law commanded, the Lord said
to divide everything we have with the poor. And he said to love
not only our neighbors but also our enemies, and to be givers
and sharers not only with the good but also to be liberal givers
toward those who take away our possessions.
Irenaeus, 130-200 AD

The rich are in possession of the goods of the poor, even if they
have acquired them honestly or inherited them legally.
John Chrysostom, 347-407

Share everything with your brother. Do not say, "It is private property." If you share what is everlasting, you should be that much more willing to share things which do not last.
The Didache

Let the strong take care of the weak; let the weak respect the strong. Let the rich man minister to the poor man; let the poor man give thanks to God that he gave him one through whom his need might be satisfied.
Clement of Rome, 1st Century

How can I make you realize the misery of the poor? How can I make you understand that your wealth comes from their weeping?
Basil of Caesarea, 330-370 A.D.

http://www.patheos.com/blogs/billykangas/2012/08/teachings-of-the-early-church-fathers-on-poverty-wealth.html

At some point these ideas moved from the religious realm into the political realm. In this book, we are trying to get our understanding and thoughts straightened out so we can see the promises of God's Word come to pass in our lives.

About eight or ten years ago I was in a meeting where the teacher said that in the dark ages, the people desperately wanted out of their poverty and serfdom. The church, which was very wealthy, did not want a lot of people striving to become clergy or priests. The landowners, who gave a lot of money to the church, did not want the lower classes striving to join their ranks. So the church taught that it was sin to try to climb out of poverty. God had put each person where he wanted them, and that if they were content in this life, their reward would come in the next life. That is where they would be rewarded. To keep the people down or content with their poverty, the church taught that to save money was sin and to have much was sin and caused by greed.

A few years later I ran across this on a web search:

In 2009 Alan S. Kahan published Mind vs. Money: The War between Intellectuals and Capitalism.

> According to Kahan, there is a strand of Christianity that views the wealthy man as "especially sinful." This brand asserts that the day of judgment is viewed as a time when "the social order will be turned upside down and... the poor will turn out to be the ones truly blessed." Many of the church fathers condemned private property and advocated the communal ownership of property as an ideal for Christians to follow. However, they recognized early on that this was an idea that was not practical in everyday life and viewed private property as a "necessary evil resulting from the fall of man."

> According to Kahan, Christian theologians regularly condemned merchants or as we would call them, wholesalers. Honorius of Autun wrote that merchants had little chance of going to heaven whereas farmers were likely to be saved. Gratian wrote that "the man who buys something in order that he may gain by selling it again unchanged and as he bought it, that man is of the buyers and sellers who are cast forth from God's temple.

> By the 11th century, Benedictine monasteries had become wealthy, owing to the generous donations of monarchs and nobility. In reaction to this wealth, a reform movement arose which sought a simpler, more austere monastic life in which monks worked with their hands rather than acting as landlords over serfs.

> By the 13th century some Dominican and Franciscan monks departed from the practice of existing religious order by taking vows of extreme poverty and maintaining an active presence preaching and serving the community rather than withdrawing

into monasteries. Francis of Assisi vowed poverty as a key element of the imitation of Christ who was "poor at birth in the manger, poor as he lived in the world, and naked as he died on the cross."

The contrast between the wealth of the church which at one point owned 20 to 30 percent of the land in Western Europe and the monks that took vows of poverty, caused some uncomfortable questions to be asked about the church's wealth.

(https://en.wikipedia.org/wiki/Christian_views_on_poverty_and_wealth)

In the book, Mind vs. Money: The War between Intellectuals and Capitalism, Kahan distinguishes three ways of holding money in disdain, "the Three Don'ts," with a fourth supplementary one thrown in for good measure. The first Don't recognizes that sufficient money is needed to live a good life but nonetheless disdains commerce:

1. "Don't Make Money (Just Have It)" (p. 31). If this mandate brings to mind Plato and Aristotle, the next has an altogether different origin.
2. "Don't Have Money (Give It to the Poor)" (p. 42) inevitably recalls the teachings of Jesus in the Gospels. Though few have been able to adhere in full to the rigors of this precept, its influence has been vast. Kahan's final Don't has a more modern ring.
3. "Don't Have or Make More Money Than Others Do (It's Not Fair)."
4. "Don't Make Money; Take It and Spend It."

Another line of Protestant thinking viewed the pursuit of wealth as not only acceptable but as a religious calling or duty. These were generally Calvinist or Puritan theologies which viewed hard work and frugal lifestyles as spiritual acts in themselves. John Wesley was a strong proponent of wealth creation. However, to avoid wealth becoming an obstacle to faith, Wesley exhorted his audiences to "earn all you can, save all you can and give away all you can." Out of that thinking comes today's prosperity theology.

(http://www.independent.org/publications/tir/article.asp?a=886)

You can see from the quotes of the early church fathers that their idea of giving it all away to be a good Christian became the doctrine of the church.

As a preacher's son I heard this expression many times, referring to the preacher, "God, you keep him humble, and we will keep him poor." To take a vow of poverty, to be poor, was considered very religious.

I have seen some people with money in the church, but mostly those without. There are many references in the Bible about trusting God. We are taught not to worry about the future, not to worry about our needs being met, not to be fearful and so on. Along this line then, some teach that it is not trusting God to save money. These people would say that you trust more in the bank and yourself in a financial emergency and your saving shows you may say you trust God with your future, but in your hearts you do not.

I heard many times the warnings from the Bible. Here are some as I remember them.

1. The love of money is the root of all evil.
2. While some coveted after, they pierced themselves through with many sorrows.
3. Give what you have to the poor and follow me.
4. Those that love silver will not be satisfied with silver...
5. Their eyes stand out with fatness; they have more than heart could wish.
6. Not given to much wine, not greedy of filthy lucre
7. Take heed, and beware of covetousness: for a man's life consisteth not in the abundance of the things which he possesseth.

I did not want to be one that was greedy or that loved money or that was pierced through, so I had decided to just live from payday to payday and trust that God would meet my needs, which He did.

But as I read His Word, I ran into verses that troubled me. For instance:

> **1Timothy 5:8-9** But if any provide not for his own, and specially for those of his own house, he hath denied the faith, and is worse than an infidel. Let not a widow be taken into the number under threescore years old, having been the wife of one man,

> **Proverbs 13:22** A good *man* leaveth an inheritance to his children's children: and the wealth of the sinner *is* laid up for the just.

> **Proverbs 21:20** *There is* treasure to be desired and oil in the dwelling of the wise; but a foolish man spendeth it up.

If we are to give everything away to the poor, and are not to save but to trust God from day to day, what do we do with these verses?

Since we have seen where some of this poverty teaching in the church came from, we will be able to see better through the haze to understand what God really expects of us in this life as we wait for the return of His son from heaven.

> *"Make all you can, save all you can, give all you can."*
> — John Wesley (1703 – 1791)

CHAPTER 4

Promises vs Warnings

Promises!

There are promises of prosperity to those that seek after God. This is an important principle to understand. As long as God comes first in your life, as long as you trust in Him, He (God) has many blessings, promises in store for you.

> **Deuteronomy 8:18 But thou shalt remember the LORD thy God**: for *it is* he that giveth thee power to get wealth, that he may establish his covenant which he sware unto thy fathers, as *it is* this day.

Notice right in the verse, the first thing mentioned is that we are to remember the Lord our God; THEN He gives the promise that it is He that gives us the power to get wealth that He may establish His covenant. This puts to bed the idea that only the poor can be followers of Christ.

Here is another promise:

> **Deuteronomy 28:2-8** And all these blessings shall come on thee, and overtake thee, **if thou shalt hearken unto the voice of the LORD thy God.** Blessed *shalt* thou *be* in the city, and blessed *shalt* thou *be* in the field. Blessed *shall be* the fruit of

thy body, and the fruit of thy ground, and the fruit of thy cattle, the increase of thy kine, and the flocks of thy sheep. Blessed *shall be* thy basket and thy store. Blessed *shalt* thou *be* when thou comest in, and blessed *shalt* thou *be* when thou goest out. The LORD shall cause thine enemies that rise up against thee to be smitten before thy face: they shall come out against thee one way, and flee before thee seven ways. The LORD shall **command the blessing upon thee in thy storehouses**, and in all that thou settest thine hand unto; and he shall bless thee in the land which the LORD thy God giveth thee.

Again we see the instruction to keep God first by the words "if thou shalt harken unto the voice of the LORD thy God."

These are promises to those who seek God first. Seek Him first, and He will prosper you tremendously.

Notice also the phrase "the Lord shall **command the blessing upon thee...**"

> **Leviticus 25:18-22 Wherefore ye shall do my statutes, and keep my judgments, and do them**; and ye shall dwell in the land in safety. And the land shall yield her fruit, and ye shall eat your fill, and dwell therein in safety. And if ye shall say, What shall we eat the seventh year? behold, we shall not sow, nor gather in our increase: Then I will **command my blessing upon you** in the sixth year, and it shall bring forth fruit for three years. And ye shall sow the eighth year, and eat *yet* of old fruit until the ninth year; until her fruits come in ye shall eat *of* the old *store*.

Notice once again the instruction to keep God first and then the phrase I will "command my blessing upon you."

"Command the blessing upon" is a rare phrase, and here it is used referring to prosperity!

It is interesting that God **could have said** He would command the blessing upon many other things, their health, their country, their children. These things **are** blessed by Him, but God reserved this phrase for commanding the blessing upon their storehouses, their prosperity. Reminds one of our opening verse: Beloved, I wish above all things that thou mayest prosper and be in health, even as thy soul prospereth. The soul prospering and the keeping God first are very similar, and both are spoken of in conjunction with prosperity. They are both part of learning how to walk with Him day by day.

> **Deuteronomy 28:11-13**   And the LORD shall make thee plenteous in goods, in the fruit of thy body, and in the fruit of thy cattle, and in the fruit of thy ground, in the land which the LORD sware unto thy fathers to give thee. **The LORD shall open unto thee his good treasure**, the heaven to give the rain unto thy land in his season, and to bless all the work of thine hand: and thou shalt lend unto many nations, and thou shalt not borrow. And the LORD shall make thee the head, and not the tail; and thou shalt be above only, and thou shalt not be beneath; **if that thou hearken unto the commandments of the LORD thy God, which I command thee this day, to observe and to do** *them:*

Here the admonition to keep God first comes at the end of the section. Look also at what else God says. God will open to you His good treasure. God has many things stored up in abundance for His children. God is a God of abundance. He is not poverty stricken Himself. He does not need to stay up at night making a new source of energy because we are about to run out. At the dawn of the industrial age, when abundant supplies of energy were going to be required to fuel it, whales were not sufficient to supply the growing need. God showed man there was oil in the ground and how to get it out. He has great storehouses or treasuries to draw from.

God promises us prosperity, that He will command His blessing upon our treasuries or storehouses. Remember prosperity or wealth is built over time. It does not just fall out of the sky like gold coins showering down upon us. (Not to say that God could not do that.) **Generally**, prosperity is built like a house, one small piece at a time like you might lay brick on a brick house. It says that through wisdom is a house built. The house we build is a house for our families. The house we build will keep God first, will trust in Him, and will see the promises of His word come to pass because we believe what He said is true and faithful.

> **Jeremiah 17:5-8** Thus saith the LORD; Cursed *be* the man that trusteth in man, and maketh flesh his arm, and whose heart departeth from the LORD. For he shall be like the heath in the desert, and shall not see when good cometh; but shall inhabit the parched places in the wilderness, *in* a salt land and not inhabited. Blessed *is* the man that trusteth in the LORD, and whose hope the LORD is. For he shall be as a tree planted by the waters, and *that* spreadeth out her roots by the river, and shall not see when heat cometh, but her leaf shall be green; and shall not be careful (anxious) in the year of drought, neither shall cease from yielding fruit.

Here we are cautioned against having our hearts depart from God. God shows us the consequences if our heart does depart, but He also gives us His will and promise. What a great promise it is! We won't even know when the droughts come because we shall still be growing and prospering. It ought to be that way, because as His sons and daughters we have a commitment to keep our Father first at all times. Therefore, His hand is upon everything we do to see it prosper. We are not alone in this process.

So these promises we are looking at are for those who trust in and seek after God and His promises.

I would like to note here also that there are many principles regarding prosperity in the Bible. It would make sense that to violate all but one and expect to see great results would not be wise.

For instance, let's say I was a giver but I was not diligent to pay attention to my business. Or I rarely thought about God or I was excessively greedy or envious or I never saved any money. Things over the long haul will not work out well. That is part of what this book is about: to learn the principles, rightly, that God has placed in His word about prosperity and incorporate them into our lives. They should be just like breathing. We learn these principles just as we learn any other subject and change our minds accordingly. Then we will have simply refined our walk with our Father.

What is a storehouse? "I will command my blessing upon your storehouses." Storehouses held hay, oats, corn, silage. They are the places where you stored the abundance that you received back from having planted a good crop. Today we have savings accounts. Droughts don't affect us as much as economic cycles do.

> **2 Samuel 6:11-12** And the ark of the LORD continued in the house of Obededom the Gittite three months: and the LORD blessed Obededom, and all his household. And it was told king David, saying, The LORD hath blessed the house of Obededom, and all that *pertaineth* unto him, because of the ark of God. So David went and brought up the ark of God from the house of Obededom into the city of David with gladness.

The presence of God was in the ark so that the man had the presence of God in his house. The Bible says we are God's dwelling place now. The reason this was written about the blessing that came upon Obededom when the presence of God was in his house was to show us what to expect in our lives as God's sons and daughters.

> **Proverbs 28:20** A faithful man shall abound with blessings: but he that maketh haste to be rich shall not be innocent.

A faithful man, one that faithfully keeps God first and is faithful to work, will abound with blessings. Do not be hasty. Prosperity is built slowly over time. Be patient.

Proverbs 8:21   That I may cause those that love me to inherit substance; and **I will fill their treasures**.

Proverbs 6:6-8   Go to the ant, thou sluggard; consider her ways, and be wise: Which having no guide, overseer, or ruler, Provideth her meat in the summer, *and* gathereth her food in the harvest.

The food the ant gathers is put into her storehouse. She saves it up.

Proverbs 10:3-4   The LORD will not suffer the soul of the righteous to famish: but he casteth away the substance of the wicked. He becometh poor that dealeth *with* a slack hand: but the hand of the diligent maketh rich.

Very interesting! It makes one wonder about those that beg along the streets. The Word tells us clearly that the hand of the **diligent** maketh rich. Go to work!!!

This may seem a little harsh.   In our culture some people beg because they are ill or can't find work for some reason and claim to be Christians and love God. That may be true. I don't know every situation, but consider this:

Psalm 37:25   I have been young, and *now* am old; yet have I not seen the righteous forsaken, nor his seed begging bread.

Proverbs 10:22   The blessing of the LORD, it maketh rich, and he addeth no sorrow with it.

One of the reasons for growing prosperity or wealth slowly over time is to give people the opportunity to learn the disciplines required to handle money. If the disciplines are not present, then the money can destroy you.

On the radio one day I was listening to a woman who had won the lottery. She shared how her family was all gone - imprisoned, hooked on drugs, and now she was divorced. She said "I had a nice family before we got all that money. The money destroyed my family; I wish we had never had it." WOW!

I watched the documentary "Broke" in which one of the players said that the money will destroy your relationship with friends, your family and ultimately your life.

God provides wisdom in His word on how to deal with prosperity so that it is a blessing to our lives.

Proverbs 13:22 A good *man* leaveth an inheritance to his children's children: and the wealth of the sinner *is* laid up for the just.

Psalm 35:27 Let them shout for joy, and be glad, that favour my righteous cause: yea, let them say continually, Let the LORD be magnified, which hath pleasure in the prosperity of his servant.

There are some who started out seeking after God and His Kingdom, but along the way, one of the things that got them off track was the deceitfulness of riches.

Mark 4:18-20 And these are they which are sown among thorns; such as hear the word, And the cares of this world, and the deceitfulness of riches, and the lusts of other things entering in, choke the word, and it becometh unfruitful. And these are they which are sown on good ground; such as hear the word, and receive *it,* and bring forth fruit, some thirtyfold, some sixty, and some an hundred.

Being deceived by the money is a problem that God mentioned back in the last book of Moses.

Deuteronomy 8:11-18 Beware that thou forget not the LORD thy God, in not keeping his commandments, and his judgments, and his statutes, which I command thee this day: Lest *when* thou hast eaten and art full, and hast built goodly houses, and dwelt *therein;* And *when* thy herds and thy flocks multiply, and thy silver and thy gold is multiplied, and all that thou hast is multiplied; Then thine heart be lifted up, and thou forget the LORD thy God, which brought thee forth out of the land of Egypt, from the house of bondage; Who led thee through that great and terrible wilderness, *wherein were* fiery serpents, and scorpions, and drought, where *there was* no water; who brought thee forth water out of the rock of flint; Who fed thee in the wilderness with manna, which thy fathers knew not, that he might humble thee, and that he might prove thee, to do thee good at thy latter end; **And thou say in thine heart, My power and the might of *mine* hand hath gotten me this wealth.** But thou shalt remember the LORD thy God: for *it is* he that giveth thee power to get wealth, that he may establish his covenant which he sware unto thy fathers, as *it is* this day.

Deceived!

Once some people have seen the prosperity of God, they get distracted by the deceitfulness of riches, or their hearts get lifted up with pride. Then they think they did it all themselves. So sad, but these are the people that the warnings are for.

As ones who seek after God first and foremost and trust in Him only, we need to be aware of the pitfalls so that we don't allow ourselves to fall into those traps.

Some stayed on track and were not distracted by the prosperity. Job comes to mind.

Warnings!

I listed for you in a previous chapter many of the warnings that I learned growing up, and I am sure many of them are familiar to you. Here they are again:

The love of money is the root of all evil. ... while some coveted after, they pierced themselves through with many sorrows. Give what you have to the poor and follow me. Those that love silver will not be satisfied with silver... Their eyes stand out with fatness, they have more than heart could wish. Not given to much wine, not greedy of filthy lucre. Take heed, and beware of covetousness: for a man's life consisteth not in the abundance of the things which he possesseth.

These are warnings or cautions to those who trust in their wealth and put money before God.

Proverbs 1:19 So *are* the ways of every one that is greedy of gain; *which* taketh away the life of the owners thereof.

Mark 10:24 And the disciples were astonished at his words. But Jesus answereth again, and saith unto them, Children, how hard is it for them that **trust in riches** to enter into the kingdom of God!

Psalm 73:3-9 For I was envious at the foolish, *when* I saw the prosperity of the wicked. For *there are* no bands in their death: but their strength *is* firm. They *are* not in trouble *as other* men; neither are they plagued like *other* men. Therefore pride compasseth them about as a chain; violence covereth them *as* a garment. Their eyes stand out with fatness: they have more than heart could wish. They are corrupt, and speak wickedly *concerning* oppression: they speak loftily. They set their mouth against the heavens, and their tongue walketh through the earth.

Proverbs 28:20 A faithful man shall abound with blessings: but he that maketh haste to be rich shall not be innocent.

This is what we have been talking about. Our life is our walk with God as His sons and daughters, doing His work to which He called us. Prosperity is part of the icing on the cake, **but it is not our life**.

Luke 12:13-21 And one of the company said unto him, Master, speak to my brother, that he divide the inheritance with me. And he said unto him, Man, who made me a judge or a divider over you? And he said unto them, **Take heed, and beware of covetousness: for a man's life consisteth not in the abundance of the things which he possesseth**. And he spake a parable unto them, saying, The ground of a certain rich man brought forth plentifully: And he thought within himself, saying, What shall I do, because I have no room where to bestow my fruits? And he said, This will I do: I will pull down my barns, and build greater; and there will I bestow all my fruits and my goods. And I will say to my soul, Soul, thou hast much goods laid up for many years; take thine ease, eat, drink, *and* be merry. But God said unto him, *Thou* fool, this night thy soul shall be required of thee: then whose shall those things be, which thou hast provided? **So** *is* **he that layeth up treasure for himself, and is not rich toward God.**

These verses are the cautions or warnings to those who put money, and their trust of money, before God. If money, prosperity or wealth becomes that important to you, then you are just feeding on the wind. In the end you have nothing.

In the following two places the Greek word for silver is used. In the first place it is called the "love of money". In the second place it is called "covetous," which means having the love of silver or money.

1Timothy 6:9-11 But they that will be rich fall into temptation and a snare, and *into* many foolish and hurtful lusts, which drown men in destruction and perdition. For the **love of money** is the root of all evil: which while some coveted after, they have erred from the faith, and pierced themselves through with many sorrows. But thou, O man of God, flee these things; and follow after righteousness, godliness, faith, love, patience, meekness.

Luke 16:14 And the Pharisees also, who were **covetous**, heard all these things: and they derided him.

These Pharisees, and those desiring to be rich referred to in these verses, loved silver more than God; they were covetous of silver.

These verses are some of the cautions or warnings against loving money more than God. God wants us to love Him first, and then He wants to prosper us and bless our treasuries, but He also tells us that if we get out of bounds, we will only hurt ourselves.

The cautions or warnings are against allowing money to go to your head once you see prosperity in your life.

Most people start at the wrong end when looking for prosperity: their job, their business, some gold mine that will make them wealthy. I propose that you start on the fundamentals and build from there. The church, because of wrong teaching, has not helped its members because the church has taught that to save is to not trust that God will meet your needs. So those in authority in the church have spent most of their teaching time on the warnings and not on the promises.

If you are broke, you need to hear about the promises of God regarding His will for you to prosper and learn how He set life up for that to happen.

Many times it is the poorest of people who think the most about money because they don't have any. This work is designed for you to sit down and rethink your finances, how you spend your money, what you spend it on, to line up your financial life more according to what God says in His Word. Then, over a period of time you can see a drastic change in your financial picture. Then, the money can lose its importance because you have the prosperity God wanted you to have. Then, it will be easier to attend upon the Lord without the distraction of money.

One of the great ways in which we can keep God first, whether we have little or an abundance, is to learn to give.

CHAPTER 5

Giving

The principle of giving is a law; it is a principle that God set up to govern life. This law of giving works for anyone whether you are a Christian, Buddhist, Hindu or atheist. It is a law. God is a giver. He so set life up that we are to follow His pattern and be givers also. Giving is a physical act. The act of giving is one of the fundamental rules of prosperity. God invented these rules, and men have discovered them by observation and have written books about these rules or laws. For example, consider the law of gravity. Newton did not invent the law; he simply observed it and then wrote the observation down. Although we could study these rules or principles or laws about prosperity from other books, it is best to go to the source. God is a giver. God set life up to operate on the principle of giving because that is what He is, and we are to follow His example.

Remember John 3:16: "God so loved the world that he **gave** his only begotten son." By the death of God's only begotten son, God was able to pay for the sins of the whole world so that all who would confess Christ as Lord and believe in their hearts that God raised Christ from the dead would be saved. God gave His son and received back millions of children. It is the principle of giving and receiving, and God shows us how it works by operating it Himself with His son. **He does not ask us to give our firstborn - only a few dollars. Nice!**

> **Philippians 4:15** Now ye Philippians know also, that in the beginning of the gospel, when I departed from Macedonia,

no church communicated with me as concerning giving and receiving, but ye only.

When we give we also receive back from God way more than we gave. Once we have given, we need to expect the promises of God to come to pass in our lives. We not only learn to give, but also we learn to expect His bounty, His abundance flowing back toward us. It is what He wants to do. It is not automatic, but it comes as we believe or expect God to bring His Word to pass in our life.

Once we incorporate this principle of giving into our lives, we should expect to see God's abundance flow back to us.

> **Luke 6:38** Give, and it shall be given unto you; good measure, pressed down, and shaken together, and running over, shall men give into your bosom. For with the same measure that ye mete withal it shall be measured to you again.

> **Proverbs 19:17** He that hath pity upon the poor lendeth unto the LORD; and that which he hath given will he pay him again.

God says that which you give; it is the same as giving it to Him, and He will repay you again. Nice! God is not a taker. If He asks you to give or to teach or minster in some capacity, He will abundantly repay you for your help and service.

> **Proverbs 11:24** There is that scattereth, and yet increaseth; and *there is* that withholdeth more than is meet, but *it tendeth* to poverty.

> **2 Corinthians 9:6-8** But this *I say,* He which soweth sparingly shall reap also sparingly; and he which soweth bountifully shall reap also bountifully. Every man according as he purposeth in his heart, *so let him give;* not grudgingly, or of necessity: for God loveth a cheerful giver. And God *is* able to make all grace

abound toward you; that ye, always having all sufficiency in all *things,* may abound to every good work:

When we learn these rules of prosperity along with the promises, we need to expect the promises of God to come to pass in our lives.

Remember:

> **3 John 1:2**   Beloved, I wish above all things that thou mayest prosper and be in health, even as thy soul prospereth.

The prospering of the soul should involve reading and studying the accounts of the Word, thinking, or pondering, or mediating on what you know from God's Word. Make the Word part of your life because of your love for God. For example, being kind, forgiving and loving one another become part of our lives as we meditate on God's love for us in Christ. As our soul prospers, our believing of God's Word increases; we learn the principle of giving and receiving, and we find it easier to prosper.

In some of the verses above, God tells us, rather implores us to give. Then He explains that we will not be poorer for doing so, for we will receive back in the same measure that we gave. If we give sparingly, we will receive back sparingly, but if we give bountifully, we will receive bountifully.

As a side note, the record in 2 Corinthians says that He makes all grace (or money, in this context) abound toward us – so we will have enough to give even more!!

We have learned that we will receive back as we give. But we also learn that if we do not give, if we withhold what is proper, that tends towards poverty.

Giving is one of the overall fundamental principles of prosperity.

What we are going to look at now is giving within the church. It is still giving but in a specific area -- in or to the church.

This form of giving is a subset of the general overall principle of giving. There do not seem to be any additional promises, except that when we stand at the bema (the judgment seat from which rewards are given at the return of Christ), this giving qualifies as walking in the love of God, according to Romans 13:1-6.

This giving is often called tithing, giving, abundant sharing, or, as in Galatians, it is called sharing fully.

Here are some verses talking about this form of giving in or to the church:
 (Technically, in the Old Testament, the temple was not called a church, but it functioned as the center of spiritual growth for God's people, similar to how the church functions today.)

> **Malachi 3:10-11** Bring ye all the tithes into the storehouse, that there may be meat in mine house, and prove me now herewith, saith the LORD of hosts, if I will not open you the windows of heaven, and pour you out a blessing, that *there shall* not *be room* enough *to receive it.* And I will rebuke the devourer for your sakes, and he shall not destroy the fruits of your ground; neither shall your vine cast her fruit before the time in the field, saith the LORD of hosts.

"Prove me" is used only here, and it is used in conjunction with prosperity.

> **Proverbs 3:9-10** Honour the LORD with thy substance, and with the first fruits of all thine increase: So shall thy barns be filled with plenty, and thy presses shall burst out with new wine.

> **Galatians 6:6-7** Let him that is taught in the word communicate (share fully) unto him that teacheth in all good things. Be not

deceived; God is not mocked: for whatsoever a man soweth,
that shall he also reap.
(Moffatt's Translation)

Galatians 6:6-7   Those who are taught must share all the
blessings of life with those who teach them the Word. Make
no mistake — God is not to be mocked — a man will reap just
what he sows;

To "communicate" simply means "to share fully". Thus it is giving in
or to the church.

Just to be clear, the word "tithe" appears only three times in the King
James Version of the New Testament: twice in the gospels and once
in Hebrews. The church epistles, Romans through Thessalonians, do
not use the word "tithe".

To distinguish between the overall principle of giving and giving to
or in the church, I have chosen to call it "giving in or to the church." It
communicates well to people, and there can be no argument over the
use of the word "tithe." Sometimes in this work, you will still see the
word "tithe," but what I mean by that is "giving in or to the church."

Romans 13:1 Let every soul be in subjection to the excelling
authorities, In fact, there is not real authority except from God,
and those that exist have been appointed by God.
(A Journey through the Acts and Epistles)

These authorities are the governing ministries in the church.

Romans 13:6 For this reason, pay tribute also, for they are
servants of God giving persistent attention to this same thing.
(A Journey through the Acts and Epistles)

The foot note on verse 6, (Pg. 248 in A Journey Through the Acts
and Epistles) is interesting: "The word *phoros* was also used to

refer to any payment. Here in Romans 13:6 and 7, it is used in a comparison to refer to that which is due to the excelling authorities mentioned in verse 1. As a citizen of Rome would pay the tribute, the custom, the respect and honor to Rome, so verses 6 and 7 speak of rendering that which is due to the excelling authorities commissioned by God."

This rendering would then be another place where God tells us to give in or to the church - those excelling authorities that govern in the church and that teach God's Word.

Since the word "tithe" is not used in the church epistles, the question arises, how much do I give to or in the church? As we read before, "Every man according as he purposeth in his heart, *so let him give;* not grudgingly, or of necessity: for God loveth a cheerful giver."

> **Romans 15:4** For whatsoever things were written aforetime were written for our learning, that we through patience and comfort of the scriptures might have hope.

> **1Corinthians 10:11** Now all these things happened unto them for ensamples: and they are written for our admonition, upon whom the ends of the world are come.

In the Old Testament times they did not have Bibles as we do. The scriptures were in the temple and perhaps the king had a copy if he made himself one as God told him to do, but the everyday person had no copies. God had many things that happened back then written down for our learning, for our admonition. We should feel greatly privileged to own a Bible and go to it daily to determine if the things we believe and are taught are so.

If we wanted to know an amount to start with for giving in or to the church, in the Old Testament they gave a tithe, or a tenth (some say that when you totaled up all they were to give it came to about 40%). Now at least we have a number. If you cannot do that much, do what you can and ask God to help you grow the amount. Remember, he that sows bountifully reaps also bountifully.

Just to clear up a point.

I have heard this question asked on a couple of occasions and never heard a good answer for it, nor I did not know what to say either. "Does it count as tithing if I give my money to someone in need? For instance, the neighbor girl is a single mom with three kids, not much money, and the tires on her car are threadbare. Can I give her my tithe?" That is a good honest question. But, I believe they are asking the wrong question. What they really want to know is: "Will God bless me back if I give her the money?" The answer is: "Absolutely, yes!" But does giving to the girl qualify as giving in or to the church as in Romans 13:1-6 and Galatians6:6-7 that we read.? The answer is, "No."

We are to have enough to give both in and to the church and to give to every good work! We should be so prosperous that we can give to every good work that we desire.

I was taught that if you were going to give, you should give it to the church and only to the church. Anything else was second rate. However, God says that He will enable us to give to every good work. Here is another verse along that line:

> **Ephesians 4:28** Let him that stole steal no more: but rather let him labour, working with *his* hands the thing which is good, that he may have to give to him that needeth.

We are to so prosper that we can give in or to the church (to those that teach and share God's Word), and we are to so prosper that we can give to those that need, and to every good work.

Now I can buy Girl Scout cookies without feeling guilty, and tip the waitress and be blessed doing it. We can also give to those that help with storm relief or for any good work we desire to give to or that God puts in our hearts, anything we know is His will, and He will abundantly bless us back financially for doing so.

When your child receives his first dollar, teach him to give part of it and to save part of it. Then teach him that God will bless him back for doing His Word. Teach this to your children.

CHAPTER 6

The Promise of Receiving & Believing

One of the main ingredients in the process of prosperity is learning that the key to receiving anything from God is believing. Believing is also translated "faith" in the New Testament, so that when you read "faith" you could read "believe" or "believing". Believing is defined as trust or confidence in information received.

Believing is the expectation that the thing promised will come to pass.

All the promises of God come to us by our believing. Most things in God's Word are not automatic. With that in mind, let's read some verses that illustrate the truth that believing is required to receive anything from God. We are doing this because later on it becomes very important in this topic we are considering.

> **Mark 9:22-24** And oft times it hath cast him into the fire, and into the waters, to destroy him: but if thou canst do anything, have compassion on us, and help us. Jesus said unto him, If thou canst **believe,** all things *are* possible to him that **believeth.** And straightway the father of the child cried out, and said with tears, Lord, I **believe**; help thou mine unbelief.

> **Mark 5:35-36** While he yet spake, there came from the ruler of the synagogue's *house certain* which said, Thy daughter is dead: why troublest thou the Master any further? As soon as Jesus

heard the word that was spoken, he saith unto the ruler of the synagogue, Be not afraid, only **believe**.

Fear and doubt are the two great enemies of believing. When and where we have fear, that fear defeats the promises of God. This is why Jesus Christ immediately responded with "be not afraid, only believe."

The other great enemy of believing or trust in God is doubt.

> **Mark 11:23-24** For verily I say unto you, That whosoever shall say unto this mountain, Be thou removed, and be thou cast into the sea; and shall not **doubt in his heart**, but shall **believe** that those things which he saith shall come to pass; he shall have whatsoever he saith. Therefore I say unto you, What things soever ye desire, when ye pray, **believe** that ye receive *them*, and ye shall have *them*.

In the following verses, these men trusted that God could heal their eyes and received some great deliverance through Jesus Christ His only begotten son.

> **Matthew 9:27-29** And when Jesus departed thence, two blind men followed him, crying, and saying, *Thou* Son of David, have mercy on us. And when he was come into the house, the blind men came to him: and Jesus saith unto them, **Believe** ye that I am able to do this? They said unto him, Yea, Lord. Then touched he their eyes, saying, According to your **faith** *(believing)* be it unto you.

The new birth, or being born from above, is received the same way, by believing.

> **Romans 10:9-10** That if thou shalt confess with thy mouth the Lord Jesus, and shalt **believe** in thine heart that God hath raised him from the dead, thou shalt be saved. For with the

heart man **believeth** unto righteousness; and with the mouth confession is made unto salvation.

Believing is a study all on its own, but this should be sufficient to understand that the promises of God come to pass as we **believe** what God has promised. We should expect to see the promises of God come to pass in our lives. Just because people should **believe** what they hear from God's Word does not mean that they will. Hebrews has an interesting comment about the people that Moses led out of the bondage of Egypt and their **believing** of the gospel they heard.

> **Hebrews 4:1-2** Let us therefore fear, lest, a promise being left *us* of entering into his rest, any of you should seem to come short of it. For unto us was the gospel preached, as well as unto them: but the word preached did not profit them, not being mixed with **faith** (believing) in them that heard *it*.

These people heard the good news of their deliverance from Egypt, all that God had done for them, and had promised to do for them. However, they did not **believe** what they heard. Since they did not **believe,** they spent 40 years in the wilderness. Their children, who did **believe** the promises, got to go into the promised land and receive all that God promised.

God is not random in the way He disperses His blessings. He is not a respecter of persons. He does not love one above another, nor is He willing to do more for one than another. The one thing that God does haverespect for is believing -- trust and confidence in what He has said.

People are pretty much the same when it comes to their children. The child who does not believe you when you tell them to be home by 10:00 has not much respect for you. But the one who believes what you have said and acts on it, generally is rewarded. First a man must believe that God is and that He is a rewarder of them that diligently seek Him (Hebrews 11:6).

When it comes to this subject of prosperity, giving and then receiving back from God, God says in Malachi to prove Him. So prove Him, and see that He will open the windows of heaven to you if you believe what He has said and act on it. If you do so, it will be life changing.

This subject of believing is integral to the next chapter, "The Storehouse Principle."

CHAPTER 7

The Storehouse Principle

I have had people ask me why they do not see prosperity even though they give in the church (which some call tithing). They give to the church but do not see the prosperity they expect. I, as well as they, have been very frustrated many times. I have also heard people say, "You are self employed, but I have a job and make the same each week. I can see how God could prosper you: He just gives you more jobs, but me, I make the same each week whether I give or not. How am I going to see the windows of heaven open?"

I never knew what the problem was until I read a book called The Storehouse Principle. Today, I think you will see the answers to both of these questions.

God did not put man on the earth to be poverty stricken. He gave Adam dominion over all the earth. That is not poor. If Adam needed anything, all he had to do was ask, and like any good father, God would have provided. God's only begotten son, Jesus Christ, never mentioned poverty as a virtue either. Contrary to what people say and teach about Jesus Christ being poor, he was not a poor man. Think about it. When Jesus was about two, the Kings of the east brought him gifts of gold, frankincense, and myrrh. We always see that picture as three men, probably because of the three gifts, and those in small boxes. But if you read about those times, when people of substance brought gifts to a king, they were not small gifts. Think about it. The night the kings left, God told Joseph in a dream to take the child and his mother to Egypt because the government was going to seek his life. What would that cost, even today, to uproot yourself in an evening and move to Europe or some other country, set up a home, and go back into business? Then a few years later God told Joseph to move back, and he had all those expenses again. God had provided Joseph with all the funds he needed the night of the first dream. In today's terms, that would have been a lot of money. This was definitely not the home of a poor man.

When you read the parables of Jesus Christ, many of them speak about a householder and his servants. He was very familiar with how those things worked. Most likely, they had servants in his home.

Poverty is not a virtue, God took care of his only begotten son. We are God's children also. Why would the Creator of the universe have His children live in poverty, or from one paycheck to the next? He would not. That is just not His way. He is a God of abundance. Those who say and teach that we are to give all our money and goods to the poor to be true followers of Jesus, wrongly understand the scriptures.

In a minute we will look at the words for "storehouse," but first think about this:

In our economy we don't have such an immediate need to save because of charities and government programs. As a country, we discourage savings by means of taxation. As people save money, we tax the interest! We tax the money when it is earned; then if any is saved, we tax the interest. We are encouraged to spend all we earn, and then to spend even more by credit. This endless cycle keeps us in debt. It reminds me of the song "Sixteen Tons" sung by Tennessee Ernie Ford.

Here are two verses from it:

> Some people say a man is made outta' mud
> A poor man's made outta' muscle and blood
> Muscle and blood and skin and bones
> A mind that's a-weak and a back that's strong
>
> You load sixteen tons, what do you get?
> Another day older and deeper in debt
> Saint Peter don't you call me 'cause I can't go
> I owe my soul to the company store

This lack of funds and debt keeps us showing up on the job to get the money to pay the debt. We have been trained to be good workers for industry and good consumers for the global economy. Someone sold us on the wrong plan.

God wants us to be God-sufficient and to have sufficiency regardless of our job. He has laid out the principles in His Word on how to do so. This is what we are looking at.

The first Hebrew word that I would like to look at is the word "asam." It is translated "storehouses" or "barns." It is used only in the plural!!!

> **Deuteronomy 28:8** The LORD shall command the blessing upon thee in thy storehouses (asam), and in all that thou settest thine hand unto; and he shall bless thee in the land which the LORD thy God giveth thee.

Notice, storehouses is plural!!!!

> **Proverbs 3:9-10** Honor the LORD with thy substance, and with the firstfruits of all thine increase: So shall thy barns (asam) be filled with plenty, and thy presses shall burst out with new wine.

Notice, barns is plural!!!!

We live in the post-industrial age, and most of us have no use for a barn or storehouse. So when we read God will fill your barns, we don't relate to it.

My grandfather on my dad's side was a dairy farmer in Wisconsin, so when this verse came up I thought about what his farm was like. He had a haymow in the top of the barn that held hay (a great place to play), a granary to hold the oats, a corn crib that held the corn, and a silo. Silos are the tall round structures that usually stand beside a barn. Some of the modern ones are blue. Silos hold silage, which is generally green chopped alfalfa. He also had a very large root cellar for potatoes, and a basement that held a ton of canned goods, mainly canned chicken. These are all storehouses. Different storehouses, or sometimes barns, for different types of things.

It is apparent in thinking about these storehouses that the farmer brought in more in the summer and fall than he could eat or use up in a week. He stored up his surplus against the long winter ahead. He used this surplus to feed his livestock so the cows could produce milk (the source of his income) all winter long until the grass turned green in the spring.

Once people moved to the city, at first they would work as they always had. They worked until they had enough to get ready for winter, and then they went home. Eventually, because of debt, they stayed in the cities year round. In 1926 Henry Ford promised them eight-hour work days and getting paid on a regular basis. That would be quite nice if you had been used to working from before dawn to after dark as a farmer, and getting paid just at harvest time. Now there was no need to store up anything. You were paid often and the city had grocery stores. You could just spend it all, and then the bankers would loan you even more to buy a house. Today, if you run out of money or food, there are food stamps!

Did farmers throughout history have food stamps for cows? If the farmer sold all his hay so he could take the kids to Disneyland in the summer, what was he to feed his cows in the winter? (Hmmm?? Pondering!!!) So, if the farmer is storing up his summer surplus against the winter ahead, is he afraid God will not supply his need when winter comes? Or, is he being wise, understanding that the seasons come in cycles—spring, summer, fall and winter?

The cycles the agricultural people had to deal with were the seasons and the weather. We are no longer so affected by either of these. Our food can be shipped in from around the world, summer or winter, but the cycles we have to deal with are of a more economic nature. Sometimes the economy is booming and sometimes it is in the cellar. Would it be wise for us to store up against the winter times of life, as the farmer did? Perhaps God gives us such an abundance so that the cycles of life need not be so dramatic for us.

<u>To be of the greatest service to Christians everywhere, this idea of giving and receiving should be taught on par with saving the surplus as it comes back to us. The reason so many believers struggle with prosperity even though they give is that the principle of saving is not taught.</u>

> **Jeremiah 17:7-8** Blessed *is* the man that trusteth in the LORD, and whose hope the LORD is. For he shall be as a tree planted by the waters, and *that* spreadeth out her roots by the river, and shall not see when heat cometh, but her leaf shall be green; and shall not be careful in the year of drought, neither shall cease from yielding fruit.

God used agricultural illustrations in His Word because that is what the people understood. We are not so much farmers, but the promises are still true for us today. Since we deal in money and not crops, we have bank accounts and not barns.

God has His own storehouses stockpiled with all kinds of treasures.

He does not have to create more because we might run out. He has huge supplies to draw from to keep man supplied.

God promises to fill our storehouses. We honour Him by keeping Him first in our lives and trusting in Him. Giving in and to the church and to those in need is one way we keep Him first, because we trust that His promises are true and that we will not be poorer for giving. We will prosper as we give.

> **Proverbs 6:6-8**   Go to the ant, thou sluggard; consider her ways, and be wise: Which having no guide, overseer, or ruler, Provideth her meat in the summer, *and* gathereth her food in the harvest.

Ants gather in much more than they need for the week, and they save it up. If you study ants, they have many different tunnels for many purposes, and at least one is for storing food. They even have tunnels to be used in case others are destroyed by little boys stomping their homes!! If part of their home is destroyed, they are immediately back out building and repairing and going about their business of storing up.

The first Hebrew word we looked at was only used twice, and both uses were plural. The next word is the word "otsar". It may be defined as "treasure, storehouse. A treasure for gold, silver, etc., a storehouse for food or drink, a treasure house, a magazine of weapons." It is used figuratively of God's armory, and it is used of the storehouses of God where He stores, among other things, rain, snow, hail, wind, sea. It is used some 70 times.

Here are some places where "otsar" is used.

> **Deuteronomy 28:12** The LORD shall open unto thee his good treasure (otsar), the heaven to give the rain unto thy land in his season, and to bless all the work of thine hand: and thou shalt lend unto many nations, and thou shalt not borrow.

Notice that we are to have such an abundance that we have no need to borrow, but that we can lend to others. We should have a surplus, more than the immediate need, and when stored for a period of time it amounts to such that we can lend.

> **2 Chronicles 32:27-29** And Hezekiah had exceeding much riches and honour: and he made himself treasuries (otsar) for silver, and for gold, and for precious stones, and for spices, and for shields, and for all manner of pleasant jewels; Storehouses also for the increase of corn, and wine, and oil; and stalls for all manner of beasts, and cotes for flocks. Moreover he provided him cities, and possessions of flocks and herds in abundance: for God had given him substance very much.

> **Proverbs 8:21** That I may cause those that love me to inherit substance; and I will fill their treasures (otsar).

God says He will fill the treasuries of those who love Him. That really is not much different from the gospels which say "seek ye first the kingdom of God and all these things shall be added unto you." Matthew 6:33

> **Proverbs 21:20** *There is* treasure (otsar) to be desired and oil in the dwelling of the wise; but a foolish man spendeth it up.

If the fool spends it all, what type of a storehouse does he have? Probably none! Don't feel bad if you do not have a storehouse; I did not have one for years either. I just did not know, and I had been taught that it was wrong to save!

Even the temple had storehouses:

> **Malachi 3:10** Bring ye all the tithes into the storehouse (otsar), that there may be meat in mine house, and prove me now herewith, saith the LORD of hosts, if I will not open you the windows of heaven, and pour you out a blessing, that *there shall* not *be room* enough *to receive it.*

As we have seen, God expects that we will have storehouses or savings accounts. He promises that if we will bring the tithes into **His** storehouse, He will make sure **our** storehouses overflow.

Part of the problem in our understanding of prosperity is our culture's perception of what wealth is. One website I read (The Art of Manliness) talked about the difference between a paycheck mentality and a wealth mentality. We relate wealth or prosperity to those who make high salaries, such as doctors, lawyers or professional athletes. If you make a million dollars a year and spend it all, are you really wealthy? No, you just live lavishly. Long term prosperity is determined by how much you save or put in your storehouse, barn, or bank. Most people do not have enough to live on for a month if they lost their job. Although prosperity covers more than just finances, if all you have saved is enough for a month, this small amount is not very prosperous.

Your paycheck is not your storehouse!!!!

Perhaps it would be best to go back to the old ways, the old paths, and build our storehouses. Today that might be translated as saving accounts. **Save some money!!!**

Another book along this line that would be valuable to read is called The Richest Man in Babylon. One of the chapters covers the idea that part of all you earn is yours to keep. Think: if you worked all your life and paid everyone else for the house, the car, the utilities, etc., and never paid yourself, is that right? The one that does all the work gets nothing? At the end of your working life, everyone else has been paid and you have nothing? That is just wrong!

Save some money!!! That is the idea behind the phrases, "thy barns shall be filled with plenty..." and "I will command the blessing upon your storehouses."

So, if the self-employed person saves part of his income, and the person drawing a paycheck saves part of his income, now we can answer the idea that, "I can see how God can prosper you; He gives you more jobs." Prosperity does not come from a job, or more jobs, or a raise, or more work, or a bigger salary, or winning the lottery. (But getting a better paying job never hurts.) Prosperity is built slowly over time by saving part of the surplus that God supplies back to us for our giving. This may take a while to wrap your mind around. **He promises to fill your storehouses. He does not promise to give you a bonus in your paycheck next week!**

Many times we look at prosperity as being able to pay this week's bills. Part of our problem is that we spend all we bring in. This is what happens to so many people that suddenly come into large amounts of money -- inheritance, lottery winners, professional sports contracts. Their habit has been to spend all they make so now they just have more to spend! The lack of knowledge of the fundamentals of prosperity causes them to lose all that they have gained. They look very wealthy and prosperous, but in the end they are worse off than in the beginning. How? The more money you have, the more you can borrow. Instead of saving money, you spend. Instead of paying cash for things, you borrow. Then, when the cash runs out, you have huge amounts of debt.

Part of understanding prosperity is understanding that we are to save part of the surplus we bring in each week. As we save, it will help to smooth out the cycles of life, and life has cycles. In the old days they saved for the winter or to help get them through droughts. Remember what we read in Jeremiah, that those who trust God will prosper even in a drought. WOW! Those storehouses helped to smooth out the cycles. Remember God said He would command His blessing upon their fields in the sixth year so they could put that surplus in storage and it would last till the ninth year?

So we should also:

Save for those slow times of the year.
Save for those large expenses.

Save for emergencies.
__Save for our retirements!__

So that we have plenty to draw on in slow times, winter times.
So that we have plenty to give to others.
So that we may be able to help in times of distress, as Joseph did.
So that we would be able to give an inheritance to our children's children and support our wives if they outlive us.

Basically God is saying today, "SAVE SOME MONEY," and He will command the blessing upon it. This saving of money is really quite different from a paycheck mentality. Our prosperity is not in our paychecks, but in what we SAVE from our paychecks. Prosperity is not so much short term as it is long term.

Remember, John Wesley said to "earn all you can, give all you can and save all you can." Some wise people, when it comes to handling money, say to: **tithe 10%, save 10%, and invest 10%.** If you do this, you are living within your means. **That answers the question about how to live within your means**.

> **In order to accomplish this, you may have to start slowly, with smaller percentages, and increase the percentages over time. You may have to restructure your expenses to accomplish that because you may have been used to consuming everything you take in each week.**
>
> **Ecclesiastes 5:11** When goods increase, they are increased that eat them: and what good *is there* to the owners thereof, saving the beholding *of them* with their eyes?

In other words, as income rises, so do our bills. As our pay goes up, we simply spend more. I remember working at a union job in Tulsa years ago. The union was negotiating for a raise of about $2.00/hour. One man I listened to already had it spent. He said as soon as the raise kicked in, he was buying a boat and making payments. He said that the payment would be just about the amount of the raise. The man thought prosperity was $2.00 per hour and a new boat! He was spending it all!

Our goal should be that our expenses rise much more slowly than our income.

An Oklahoma football player, Ryan Broyles, recently signed a four year $3.6 million contract with the Lions with a $1.2 million signing bonus. He stated that he and his family will live on $60,000/year. The rest will go into the bank. He did not come up with this way of dealing with money on the spur of the moment. Somewhere along the line he learned and instilled within himself the fundamentals of prosperity. Then, when a large amount of money did come his way, those disciplines of finances protected him.

We should expect to see the promises of God come to pass in our lives by believing and by being obedient to His Word. If the material things become more important than God, then the cautions and warnings kick in. Keep God first and trust only in Him.

> **Proverbs 24:3-4** Through wisdom is an house builded; and by understanding it is established: And by knowledge shall the chambers be filled with all precious and pleasant riches.

CHAPTER 8

Saving Money

Now that we have seen this storehouse principle, let's think about what we have learned.

1. First of all in order for the storehouse principle to work in our lives, we need to become givers ourselves.
2. God expects us to save the surplus.
3. God expects that we have a barn, storehouse or bank to put the surplus in.
4. God expects that we do not spend all we make.
5. This is more of a long term, net worth prosperity rather that just enough to make the next house payment.
6. This saving of the surplus should be taught whenever giving and receiving is taught.
7. The self-employed and the wage earner can both save a surplus, and thus God prospers both.
8. The storehouse principle applied begins to move us from the realm of consumers to the realm of producers.

Let's look at these one at a time:

1. First of all, in order for the storehouse principle to work in our lives, we need to become givers ourselves.

Giving is a great sign of the trust we have in God in our heart. We trust that His word is true, and that He will bless us back abundantly if we give. I have known many people over the years who did not give. Most eventually disappeared off the map of those involved in the things of God. Believing is a matter of the heart. Giving is an outward recognition of God's abundant supply in our lives—that He is our sufficiency.

I knew a man about my own age many years ago who came to me and told me he had stopped giving in and to the church. He told me that he hadn't given anything in three months. He said, "I still make as much money as when I gave, and all my bills are paid. This whole thing on giving is a farce."

We do not validate or invalidate God's Word by our experiences. God's Word is much more reliable than a two or three-month experiment on prosperity. The Bible says "God is not a man that He should lie." (Numbers 23:19) But this is the problem: If you think the prosperity should come through your paycheck as he did, then you can end up deceived or frustrated. The promises of prosperity are always true because God promised them and He will bring His promises to pass in our lives as we believe them.

He needs people who are willing to give. The Church needs money to operate on. Where is that to come from? God blesses those back that give in or to the church. We have read the promises. God also needs people who will open their hearts and wallets to those in need. Remember the phrase, "have to give to him that needeth." For those who are able (that is what this book is about) and willing (that is a matter of the heart), God will repay more than what you gave to help.

Note: He does not ask us to give it all, just part.

2. God expects us to save the surplus.

God does not command us to save some money, but you can clearly see from the scriptures that He expects that we will save the surplus.

With phrases like "fill your barns," "oil and wine in the house of the wise," "fill your treasuries," we should structure our finances so that we can save the surplus that He supplies. This is why we covered in a previous chapter the principle of believing. If you believe that He will fill your treasuries, you will have no problem restructuring your spending so that you can see His supply.

3. God expects that we have a barn, storehouse, or bank to put the surplus in.

Since that is what He expects us to do, we should be ready to receive what He sends our way and make a place to put it. This is another reason we covered the topic of believing. Many of us have believed what God said about giving, and we gave. Some of us have also believed that God would give back to us, and we received that. We should also then believe that He expects us to have storehouses, a place to save part of that surplus, rather than just spending that surplus as a "good consumer". We should have different accounts with appropriate names in which to put that surplus.

4. God expects that we do not spend all we make.

We may have been used to spending it all; I was, but that is simply a choice. We may have to go over our finances and restructure them to retain some of that surplus He promises. For some, this may involve getting out from under massive debt. If we believe what we have been reading, we must realize that if we head in the direction of God's Word, He will be right there to help us. Getting started is always the hardest part, as it involves changing the mind and the habits, but the rewards are great.

5. This is more of a long term, net worth, wealth prosperity rather that just enough to make the next house payment.

If we do not save part of what we make, how are we to see His prosperity, especially over the long haul, 20 years down the road? If our prosperity comes in our paycheck each week, does He just increase our paychecks each week because we gave the week before? Each time we give do we get a bonus? He gives us a bonus because we gave, so then we give even more and now we get a bigger bonus? Where will that stop? Remember, prosperity is more in saving the surplus than in getting a raise.

6. This saving of the surplus should be taught whenever giving and receiving is taught.

Whenever we teach giving and receiving and leave off the part about saving money, that benefits the church or those in need, but it shortchanges the person giving. Unless the person giving understands that there will be a surplus coming back AND that they are to save it, they will have a difficult time seeing the promises of prosperity over the long run. As I said before, I have heard people talk about giving and giving, and yet they just don't see the prosperity. **We need to teach them to save!**

7. The self-employed and the wage earner can both save a surplus. God prospers both.

Because we now understand that the prosperity that God has promised is to come from saving part of the surplus coming back to us, that gets rid of the question of the difference between the self-employed and the wage earner. Really cool!

8. The storehouse principle applied, begins to move us from the realm of consumers to the realm of producers.

If you remember when the economy tanked in 2008, people began saving their money and paying off their debts instead of spending, because they were unsure about the future. Most of the financial channels on the television were constantly talking about how or when the consumer was going to come back into the market. Our economy is a consumer-driven economy. We see it all around us—BUY, BUY, BUY. When we run out of money, we put it on a credit card so we can buy some more. God is showing us that instead of buying, spending, and consuming so much, He wants us to become savers. Once we have been saving for awhile, the next concern is what to do with this money. Banks pay only a small interest rate, so we have to look for ways to cause those accounts to grow. Some people buy restaurants, some people flip houses, some people trade cars, and so forth. These endeavors are producing rather than spending. Decide today to leave the consumer market and become a saver and producer with the prosperity that God supplies you with.

Remember the story of the Good Samaritan? He found the man beaten and wounded on the side of the road. He bound up the man's wounds and took him to the inn. Then he told the innkeeper he would pay him back whatever was necessary when he returned. This man was one who did not spend all he took in. He had saved some of it. In our times we would have taken the man to the hospital. Have you ever seen a hospital bill for a several day stay? Outrageous! The Good Samaritan not only had the willingness to help, but also he had the ability. He was a prosperous man, one who had to give to him that needeth. God needs people such as this today also.

Remember to never argue with people over this subject. Some just don't want to give. They never have given and probably never will. It is just the way they are. Some of those that don't give find it easier to say that **YOU** should give it all away because they believe that much prosperity is sin. It's easier for them to tear you down or accuse you than for them to rise up in their believing and see the abundance God has promised in the lives of those who give. If they can drag you down to their level, then they do not look so bad. Pray for them that God would open their eyes.

Financial Disciplines

1. *Don't Spend*
2. *Keep Saving*

3. *Guard Savings with Prayer*
4. *Don't Borrow*
5. *Trust God is Your Partner*
6. *Diversify (Ecclesiastes 11:2)*

Ecclesiastes 11:2 Give a portion to seven, and also to eight; for thou knowest not what evil shall be upon the earth.

What would you attempt to do if you knew you could not fail?

CHAPTER 9

The Comfort Zone

"Move out of your comfort zone. You can only grow if you are willing to feel awkward and uncomfortable when you try something new." Brian Tracy

Changing our habits is a growing process, and many times this causes us anxiety because we are learning to live outside of our comfort zone. We are unsure how it will work out for us as we move up to a new level in our believing and in our lives.

Some adults say that it is too hard and just won't do it. Some start out fine, but then quit in a week or two. We should adopt the same attitude as the kids.

Have you ever watch a child take blocks out of a box and put them on the floor, then take the blocks off the floor and put them in the box? Over and over and over. As adults we tend to think, isn't once enough to learn that process? But not a child. He will keep at that, out of the box, onto the floor, off the floor, into the box, until he has learned what is necessary. Research shows they have some anxiety, but once they learn whatever is there to learn, the anxiety goes away.

My oldest daughter said that her oldest daughter kept her up part of the night once pacing back and forth on the bed. She understood the youngster was obviously processing something mentally. She said after that night my granddaughter used her pronouns much better. Her mind was processing the pronouns I, mine, you, and yours, and others.

We might experience anxiety also as we learn new skills in our jobs, in dealing with our children, in handling our marriage; so it is with our finances. These principles we have been talking about are opportunities for growth. We can either learn to handle more or walk away and stay at the same level. We are learning about giving in or to the church and in other areas, and we are learning about saving. We need to be like a small child, and not quit until we get to the new level.

Once we work our way through these things, by changing our minds, reorganizing our finances, and making some decisions on what direction we are heading, we will find that, over time, we are able to handle more and more. Then that which once made us uncomfortable and caused us anxiety, will become normal.

It is always possible to change, or else God would not ask us to renew our minds and change our thinking.

We received much of our mental programming about finances from our families. Some people learned well how to deal with money in the family in which they grew up. Some did not. Perhaps many did not. Many people are going to depend on their social security checks for their retirement income. Why? They never learned these essential principles of handling money.

Someone told me the other day that they do not ever remember talking about prosperity as a family, yet they knew many of the rules of prosperity. It is the way they grew up.

We may not have grown up that way, so we may have to change our minds, grow up a level or two, and experience a little anxiety to acquire new prosperous habits.

Famous people have had to learn how to handle their finances also. I remember hearing recently that when Shaquille O'Neal became a professional ball player, he spent a million dollars the first day. WOW! His banker called and told him that he needed to get some education on money, or he was going to go bankrupt as about 70% of all other professional athletes do. Well, Shaq listened, grew, and got out of his comfort zone. When he retired from basketball he received a doctor's degree in education and had many investments.

The reason 70% of professional sports figures are bankrupt within five years of retirement is that they have never learned what we are looking at in this book. These principles are the fundamentals to prosperity. Those sports figures grew up spending all their income. So when that income drastically increased, they spent a lot more. They were not more prosperous, just living lavishly.

The fundamental principles of money are in God's Word. Does He teach you how to keep books or how to operate a QuickBooks program? No! For that you have to read other books.

Once you learn about giving and saving, we can learn from other great books that people have written in our day and time to help us straighten out our messes.

For instance, if you have a lot of debt, Dave Ramsey has several great books for that.

> **Proverbs 21:5-6** The thoughts of the diligent *tend* only to plenteousness; but of every one *that is* hasty only to want. The getting of treasures by a lying tongue *is* a vanity tossed to and fro of them that seek death.

We learn that we need to be diligent in our business and financial matters, and that diligence tends toward having plenty. Obviously, this must be a slow process because God says that if you are hasty you will lose what you have. Lying also is not helpful. We need only to trust our Father and apply His principles diligently, and that will work well. Don't be in a hurry. You will see the results in time.

> **Proverbs 21:12** The righteous *man* wisely considereth the house of the wicked: *but God* overthroweth the wicked for *their* wickedness.

The wise watches and sees what is the end of the wicked. You can find many examples of these unwise people in the pages of the Bible and in life. The wise learn from the mistakes they see others make, and they don't copy them.

> **Proverbs 21:17** He that loveth pleasure *shall be* a poor man: he that loveth wine and oil shall not be rich.

You may have to curb some of your appetites and save that money instead. It pays off well in the long run.

> **Proverbs 21:20** *There is* treasure to be desired and oil in the dwelling of the wise; but a foolish man spendeth it up.

Once again God exhorts us to SAVE SOME MONEY!! If we learn to be faithful in that which God blesses us, He will grant us even more. We will read some more about that later on. Treasure and oil—we might say, the house is paid off, the emergency fund is fully funded, and the investments are doing well because we learned **not to spend all the surplus.**

> **Proverbs 21:25-26** The desire of the slothful killeth him; for his hands refuse to labour. He coveteth greedily all the day long: but the righteous giveth and spareth not.

The lazy have great desires for prosperity, but they are not willing to do the work to see it come to pass. God says the righteous giveth and spareth not. The righteous is one that trusts God, and works, and gives, and saves. Cool!

They don't give it all away, but they don't spend it all either!!

I remember hearing, "Give only to the best causes, to those that move the Word." I adhered to that to the end that I did not tip the server, buy Girl Scout cookies, or give to any other cause. I always felt bad, though.

> **2 Corinthians 9:6-8** But this *I say,* He which soweth sparingly shall reap also sparingly; and he which soweth bountifully shall reap also bountifully. Every man according as he purposeth in his heart, *so let him give;* not grudgingly, or of necessity: for God loveth a cheerful giver. And God *is* able to make all grace abound toward you; that ye, **always having all sufficiency in all** *things,* **may abound to every good work:**

Why should I as a Christian be labeled a skinflint? I should, as a Christian, have enough to tip or buy cookies. I should have enough to give to every good work that is in my heart to do.

I found that giving in this manner really opened up my life. I just felt better. It was not rebellion against what I had learned but learning to see and believe what was written. That always works. It is a pleasure to give to others. I think the Master once said it is more blessed to give than to receive. Try it.

God's Word is filled with great knowledge and wisdom on how to live. To rise up to that level may take some diligent work. This means every week making sure you are doing what He said and expecting to see the promises of His Word come to pass until it becomes a habit or second nature.

My wife and I try to go over our progress every Monday night, but usually it is once a month. The reason we sometimes miss discussing this weekly is that we did not do it for the first 40 years, but we are making progress. The last three or four years we have beat out what we did in the first 40. Amazing what applying God's Word can do when we believe in it and do it.

This growth is not without anxiety at times, and some crying (not me). But, once you see for yourself how well it works, I believe you won't go back.

You will have to get out of your comfort zone. I had a woman tell me that when I first taught this information, their family had about $250.00 in the bank. They have small children, too. She said she opened up a savings account for every member of their family and deposits to them regularly, and **nobody** spends that money. She said it was amazing how much was in those accounts in two or three years. Now her problem is what to do with the money. She said it changed her life. She won't go back to spending it all.

It may not be comfortable at first, but new things rarely are. If God expects us to do these things, we should just do them and ask Him for help in understanding, expecting that He will bless our endeavors. This giving and saving may cause some anxiety, but we will get used to it if we stick to it.

We can overcome the incorrect programming. Learn the discipline of handling money. We need to step out of that comfort zone and grow into a new higher level. Once we get used to this level, we will have a new comfort zone. Then, attack the next level.

CHAPTER 10

Funding vs. Savings Accounts

We had saved some money in the past. Usually the amount got to about $5,000.00, and then it would be gone for a down payment on a truck or some other legitimate purpose. Every time this happened, I felt a little sick inside because it was now all gone, but I did not know what to do.

Then one day I learned that many people have a subconscious limit as to how much they are comfortable handling or having. If they acquire more than that, they will just get rid of it. This is why lottery winners at times have been known to leave a briefcase of money in a taxi cab. They are out of their comfort zone with the money, and their mind is trying to get back to where they are comfortable.

When I learned this I knew my limit was $5,000.00. I thought, "That is disgusting!" So we opened several accounts, and I told my wife I do not want to know how much is in them until we are way past $5,000.00. That worked. I could not believe I was so small minded. WOW!!! Don't tell anyone; I would be embarrassed.

One of the things we discovered was that the saving accounts had no named purpose, so the first time something came up that was needed, we spent it on that and it was all gone.

Well, there is a much better way.

At first we started a journal, and named the accounts, and decided how to fund each. For instance, we started an emergency fund. That was a great encouragement for the establishment of other accounts. We have used the emergency fund several times.

I had also always wanted to save my change in a big water bottle, but I did not have one, so I used quart jars. At that time, we were still constantly short of funds, but I would not let my wife use the money in the jars. I had begun to realize there had to be a better way than constantly having to spend the money I had saved to pay a bill. God would provide some way other than cashing in those jars. He did.

When we took a trip to Israel a few years later, those jars provided our spending money -- $800.00. No borrowing; it did not come out of the checking account, no credit cards. Just cash. I think that was the turning point for my wife in the saving of change.

Since that time we have found excuses to put extra money in those jars. (Now we use large plastic coffee containers because she dropped an empty quart jar in the bank and made a mess.) When we sold things we weren't using from the storage building, that went into the jar. We have used the money in that jar to give my youngest daughter money for clothes for her honeymoon, to give my oldest son money for a nice suit for a job interview; to buy a computer, a new camper shell for my wife's truck, a new bed, a sewing machine, and other things. It is also amazing that once this became part of our lives, how much faster the money came back after we spent it. At first $300.00 in the jars seemed like a lot. Now it commonly comes in around $2,000.00. Amazing!! God is good!!

It was especially nice that the purchase of these things has never affected our checking account, nor did we use a credit card. We felt no financial effect at all; all from saving change and finding excuses to save. I have seen people throw their change away. Not good stewardship!

We thought we were saving about 10% of our income. As we sat down and were looking at what we were doing one night, I realized that some of what we were saving was money saved to buy things in the future: car replacement, gifts, vacations, etc. This was not truly a savings account. My wife started to cry. "WE call it a savings account and THE BANK calls it a savings account." I said, "I know, but we are just saving up to buy things!" Once the shock was over, we decided to rename the accounts funding accounts.

We already had an account for our business called a funding account. We ran into trouble in our business checking account several years ago because of negative balances on paper. There was plenty in the account, but the balance we saw was negative because of the way we kept track of the funds. We had many large bills to pay each year. Finally, we took all of our large business bills, totaled them up, divided by 12, and put that much money in a separate funding account every month to fund those bills. That has been a wonderful way of dealing with the large bills. The account never had much in it, but it usually had enough to pay the next large bill. When the bill was due, we transferred the amount to the regular account, and paid the bill.

Then we found that actual savings was around 5% in our personal accounts, so we fixed that immediately.

Now, savings for future purchases are called funding accounts—like a car fund or a vacation fund, for example. The "saving accounts" are actual savings accounts. The money in the savings accounts is never spent except to buy and resell for a profit. Then the money is replaced into the savings account after giving some in and to the church or to some other need.

I have had people tell me that as they started their emergency account, they kept having emergencies come up that would drain it. We had that problem in the beginning, too.

> **James 4:7** Submit yourselves therefore to God. Resist the devil, and he will flee from you.

If you just keep at it and pray, eventually the emergencies will quit. **Just keep at it. Don't give up.**

We are looking at the long term effects of having specific types of accounts. We may have weeks where it seems to go backwards, but if we keep up the savings over our lifetime, it will be amazing. It will be like God has opened the windows of heaven.

So, we have an emergency account. It is not fully funded with six months of income replacement, but we are getting there. Once that account is fully funded, the money that now goes into it will go to another fund, or into savings.

In one bank account we have savings for vehicle replacement, gifts, vacation, warranty, food storage, and remodeling. Our warranty plan is the following: instead of buying the extended warranties stores offer on most products, we decline and put that amount into the warranty fund. Then, when an item breaks down, a new one is purchased from the warranty fund.

Since these funds are all in the same bank account, we needed a way to easily keep track of how much was in each. We used a spreadsheet and found a template for it that works beautifully. It allows us to deposit, for example, $100.00 and it automatically divides it between the different savings categories, according to the percentage we decide each account receives. We also put a limit on each account so we would know when it was fully funded. The template allows us to change the percentage very easily on each account, so that when one is fully funded the money goes to another account. Very nice!

http://www.vertex42.com/ExcelTemplates/savings-goal-tracker.html

We have found that having the money in different banks has the advantage that it takes a few days to transfer from one bank to another, and that cuts down on the possibility of cheating. We try to limit ourselves to spending only what is in each fund, no mixing or borrowing from one fund to another.

If the money is just in a big pile, and it is not predetermined what it is for, it will get spent on the first item that comes along. This procedure stops some of that. Also, if you need more than what is in that account, pray. Ask God to help you fund that account fully.

I had to get over the idea that if I had any money at all it was wrong to ask God for more until I had used up that I had. As I learned in the book, *The Storehouse Principle*, we should not start praying when we hit the bottom of the barrel. We try to have the barrel overflowing, and when we get even with the top, we pray for more.

If God expects you to spend every dime you have to meet a need before He will give you more, then there is no reason for different accounts or storehouses. He says He will fill your treasuries. Plural. Just get used to praying and asking Him to help you, and expect Him to provide.

If you build the disciplines into your life on smart money management, the disciplines will protect you. After having done this work with these accounts, it has helped us to see money in a bigger way.

We decided what accounts we wanted to have for savings and how we were going to fund them. Some are automatic transfers. These are about 10% of our income.

Once you have disciplined yourself to following a regimen of saving, and saving to fund future purchases, this habit gives you a great sense of freedom, and it takes much of the pressure off your mind about being able to pay your bills. This will help you to attend upon the things of God without so much financial distraction.

> **A Chinese proverb says that saving money is like taking a five-gallon bucket to the seashore and using a teaspoon to fill it. Spending money is like pouring the water into the sand.**

CHAPTER 11

Practical Suggestions

Remember, some people, rather than doing the work of learning about prosperity and rising up in their believing and understanding, find it easier to drag you down to their level of unbelief; then they don't look so bad. They will say, "See, he could not do it either;" "giving was under the law;" "it did not work for him." You come to realize that no matter what you teach them, they just do not want to do this stuff. Don't argue with them; just let them be.

This is why sometimes it is best to keep your believing to yourself. Many times you might take a lesson from the book, *The Millionaire Next Door*. If you have believing, have it to yourself before God.

Monitor your accounts every week to see growth or holes in your bag.

Checking your accounts:
Sit down once a year and examine all that you are paying for.
　　Can you get rid of it?
　　Can you reduce the price?
　　Can you get it cheaper somewhere else?
　　(We have called our insurance agent several years in a row because of increases and in some cases saved some money.)

Never say, "It's just five dollars":
Some bills come in with all types of charges enumerated on the bill. You may or may not need to pay those. You may be paying for things you are not even using. In some cases, you may be erroneously

charged for things you don't owe. Many years ago, a utility company where I live consistently overcharged people three or four dollars every month for some "line" item. Eventually, they got sued and had to pay back millions of dollars to their clients. What may be five dollars to you, multiplied by hundreds of thousands of people made some companies a lot of money. If you don't understand the charge, call them up ask them what it's for or why you have to pay that. It's called being diligent or good stewardship.

Married couples:
If you're married, you need to work on the principles of prosperity together. It works the best if the husband and wife are on the same page. Do it together. Read this book and other books together and discuss what you are learning. You can help and encourage each other with your understanding and with what God's Word says on the topics.

Gifts:
Some people give stock certificates as presents to their children and grandchildren rather than trinkets that soon break. They do this because they have a long term perspective on life. Some people live from one paycheck to the next financially. Some live year to year, but others see down the generations until Christ returns.

Fear:
One reason people are tight with their money is fear, pinched thinking. You overcome fear by putting the Word in your mind. Some of the ways this fear manifests itself are the following:

1. A fear of going broke which is a failure to believe that God will prosper them
2. A fear of being wasteful or greedy
3. A fear that they won't have enough to pay their next large bill, so they do without, or they don't tip, or they buy cheap, or they don't pay current small bills out of fear that they won't be able to pay the next large one, or they don't give much.

Ask yourself, where these fears and thoughts come from, and then correct them.

If our Father is a God of abundance, and His Word clearly states that He is, then why should we ever suffer any lack? It's only because of our own pinched, limited thinking and our own believing. We simply don't trust that He will do what He has said.

Once you recognize this, if you have that problem, then go to work. Put God's Word in your mind: "My Father owns the cattle on a thousand hills." Psalm 50:12. "Beloved, I wish above all things..." 3 John 1:2. You say to your mind, "This is our new standard." "It may be uncomfortable at first, but this is how I am going to conduct my life." When the thought or the feeling comes, "You won't have enough," just say, "The Lord will provide."

Be judicious:
You can't spend your money buying a Porsche if you just lost your job. But many times, that is not the case. For us in the past, we've had the money to pay the bill, but for fear of not being able to pay the next large bill, we put off paying this one as long as possible, even though we had the money. I don't know what the principle is called, but if you want to get filled again, first you have to empty yourself.

If you have the money, just pay the bill. Then pray and ask Him to help with the next one coming up. Some people pray for funds ahead of time. Some people expect God to keep their families from even getting sick. **Go on the offensive.**

You have to use some common sense. You can't acquire the bills of the upper middle class and try to pay them on a ditch digger's salary. Many times I believe our biggest problem lies in not expecting to see God bring His Word to pass. It's our thinking that has to change first, how we see ourselves in our mind's eye. Make up your mind. Instead of seeing yourself and confessing with your mouth that you never have enough, decide to become a giver, as God's Word says. Decide to believe God's Word that He is able to make all grace abound toward you. All grace abounds toward you, so that you having all sufficiency in all things, may abound toward every good work.

So, when you study or read God's Word, look for verses or records that talk of God's abundance and prosperity.

Did He prosper people in the Old Testament?
> To what degree did He do that?
> Was He stingy or tight?
> Or was He abundant in meeting their needs?

In 2 Kings 3:1-7 there is a record of the woman who poured out the oil to pay off her debts. Did He give her just enough to pay off the debts? The answer is no; He gave her a fully funded retirement **on top of** the debt payoff. She did not even ask for that.

He did that for her, and she was a servant. We are sons and daughters. We should be able to expect to see His abundance in our lives also.

So grab a hold of the helm of the ship of your life and steer your thoughts into alignment and harmony with what God has promised.

In this way you will get rid of your pinched thinking. You will practice the principles in the Word and become a giver, become a tither.

Just tell your stubborn brain, "We will go in the direction of God's Word. God said it; I believe; He'll bring it to pass. I have trusted Him with my eternal life. I trust Him with a portion of my time every week. Just as when I speak in tongues and interpret, I trust He'll have the words right there because that's what He promised in His Word. Similarly, I will also become a giver, and I trust He'll bring His Word to pass by making all grace abound toward me in my life right now. Since He is faithful in these other areas, and I know He is, then I trust He'll be faithful in the area of giving and receiving, too."

Economics is not a zero sum game.
A zero sum game is one where in order for **me** to receive more **you** have to have less. If that was true, who was the loser when God filled the woman's pots with oil? God did not take from anyone to give that to her. That is why we call it a miracle. No, economics is not a zero sum game. As we labor, we add value into the economy, and we are paid for our labor. Sometimes our labor produces products out of raw materials. Those products, with our labor added in, are worth far more than the raw materials.

Attitudes
With money, attitudes make a large difference. Consider the following: You are out of town and become stuck there and need a hotel room. Your mind may say, "I can't spend the money on a hotel room. I can't. I need that money for something else." It causes a lot of angst in your life. However, if you took the attitude, "I am glad I have the money, so I will get the room and things will work out. God will supply," you relieve yourself of so much mental pressure, and then things just work better.

Paying off debt
There is a difference between paying off debt and saving money. It seems like you're getting ahead in both cases, but technically, one is actually buying something and the other is saving. **It's not the same thing.** It may even make more sense to pay off the debt **before** you save because of the interest you owe on the debt. BUT once that debt is paid off, you're still broke. You just don't owe as much. **However,** if you save the money, you have something to invest; you have something for your labor. Saving part of your income is a great habit, and it does something for your self image to have money in the bank that you have saved. It is just different. Try it. Pay off that debt, but save at the same time, so that by the time the debt is paid off you are well into the habit of saving.

Finding excuses to save
You have to find excuses or reasons to save your money. Saving is

more than just not buying. Saving is putting it in a bank account with no intention of spending it. You could save unexpected money, for instance, extra work on a Saturday, checks for your birthday, or extra money that was left in the checking account at the end of the week or month, or anything else unexpected. First, give from those funds, and then save the rest. Even though we called them funding accounts, in order to fund them, we have to save. You can also find ways to put money in your funding accounts—money from garage sales you run, things you sell on E-Bay, change stored in a jar, things you're not using that you can sell, whatever you can come up with. Find ways to put money in those funding accounts. Get an extra job if you need to temporarily. Become a saver or producer, not a consumer.

We noticed that if the extra is put into the checking account, it is just gone. If we save it, we don't miss it. Interesting!

See if that happens for you, too.

What are your needs?

Philippians 4:19 But my God shall supply all your **need** according to his riches in glory by Christ Jesus.

Some have said that anything over your need is greed, and that God will not supply that greed. That would make sense, but then the questions begin. Do you really need a three-bedroom home; could you get by with a two-bedroom home? If company comes to town, put them in a hotel. Perhaps you don't need a house at all, but could you suffice with an apartment? Could you choose a cheaper part of town to live in? On and on.

Do you really need two cars? …. You could both take the bus. Would you really need that many clothes, if you washed more often?

If you compare yourself with Christians that live in third world countries then you could think about this: They live in mud huts, and you can't do with an apartment and think you need a house—with how many bedrooms? and look at the size of that kitchen!!

There is no end to this kind of questioning and thinking. You could literally pare yourself down to living in a cave with only a loin cloth.

I once was driving with a group of Christians through a very nice neighborhood. The houses were probably in the range of $7-800,000 twenty years ago. Someone in the car said: "That has to be nothing but pure greed to live in a house like that." Really? I did not know what to say at that time, so I just kept quiet.

If it is greed to own an $800,000 home, is $500,000 OK? Where is the line drawn? Who gets to decide whether a certain purchase or item is greed or need? There is no answer to this line of thinking.

Maybe this whole line of thinking is outside the bounds of God's Word to begin with. It is mostly looking at what someone else has and judging whether you think that is their need or greed.

Consider this: once you have done what God says to do according to His word as regards giving and saving, then the rest is yours to do with as you please. You have done your duty, so to speak. Then if you want to build an $800,000 house, go for it. Remember Solomon in the Old Testament? God gave him great wisdom and riches. The Bible says that in Solomon's days, gold and silver were as plentiful as stones in Jerusalem.

Apparently he did not save ALL the riches God gave him. He was not like the king sitting in his counting house, counting all his money! He built many great works and paid the craftsmen and prospered them in the process.

What do you really need?
- You need what God has promised in His Word.
- You need to be able to do what He gives you as a responsibility.

- You need to provide for your family.
- You need to have enough to give in or to the church.
- You need to have to give to every good work and to those in need.
- You need to provide your wife a retirement for as long as she lives (in other words, have enough to put quite a bit in savings each week).
- You need to have enough to give an inheritance to your children's children.

That is a lot more than a loin cloth in a cave. Sometimes what you need is a better paying job. Some may need to send their children to a private school. As I heard someone say, "You need to get your needs up!" You may need to get some more education so you can bring more value to the market place. We are paid for the value we bring to the market.

Learning to say, "No!"
Once you have saved up some money, you have to get good at saying, "NO!" Things will come up to spend the money on. Say, "No." There has to be a better way. Ask God to show you how else to get that done without spending that money. What good does it do to save for two years and see it all disappear and then do it again? It is very disheartening. You have to have the mindset that this is not the way God designed life. There has to be a better way to live life than to constantly give away our hard earned cash to some emergency or to borrow to meet our needs. Ask God, "What can I do?" Then read some books on how people managed their money. Start an emergency account and some funding accounts, and then limit yourself to just what is in those accounts to spend. Learn to hold a tight rein on your money.

Find some other way to pay:
Find some other way to pay for things than to pay cash or write a check or put it on a credit card. Is there something you can sell or trade? Ask God, "How can I do this without dipping into my savings?" Ask God, "How do I buy a house? How do I go to college?"

Don't borrow the money to go to college; find someone that will pay for it for you. Look for scholarships. Go to the college and ask them where to go look for the money without borrowing it. Go to the department of your major and ask how to get scholarships to that department. Make up your mind that you are not going into debt for a college education. Get a job working for a company where one of its perks is paying for college.

Seek the blessor, not the blessing:
This has been a stock answer I have heard given in the past to those who do give and just don't seem to see the prosperity they might expect. It implies that the giver is more interested in the money than in walking with God. It implies that we should give with no thought about the blessing coming back. If God did not want us to have any concern about the surplus coming back to us, why does He spell it out over and over in His Word? I believe this answer was given because of a lack of understanding that God expects us to save the surplus as it comes in and that we are to so set up our finances that we can see and save that surplus. That stock answer tends to keep the money flowing, but the giver gets less than they should expect. We should expect to see God keep His Word, and He does. As we rise up and save that surplus, we will see our Father bring His word to pass in our lives, and have an even greater walk with the blesser and have the blessing too!

> **Luke 11:9** And I say unto you, **Ask, and it shall be given you; seek, and ye shall find; knock, and it shall be opened unto you.**

These are principles that God honors. Remember, He is able to do exceeding abundantly above all we can ask or think. (Ephesians 3:20)

CHAPTER 12

You Are Not Alone

James 1:5-6 If any of you lack wisdom, let him ask of God, that giveth to all *men* liberally, and upbraideth not; and it shall be given him. But let him ask in faith, nothing wavering. For he that wavereth is like a wave of the sea driven with the wind and tossed.

As God's children, we have some great avenues available to us for learning and protection. Here God says that if you lack wisdom, which we all do, all we have to do is ask, expecting that He will hear us and grant us the wisdom we seek.

We have a great book of financial wisdom available to us in God's Word. We have seen much of that wisdom already in what we have been looking at so far. This wisdom on how money works rightly is priceless. Once you understand how true prosperity works in life, you can do it over and over again. For instance, if you lose it all, you can with the wisdom you have learned, do it over again. This is why God's Word says that wisdom is more valuable than money.

Someone once asked me, "If I put my money in the stock market and lose it all, what happens then?" I told them, "Well, it depends on your motivation in becoming prosperous." If you were just after the money and you lose it all, those are the people that jump out the 10th story windows, as in the stock market crash of 1929. But, if your motivation in becoming prosperous was to see God's Word come to pass, you are in much better shape. If you became a giver and a saver because you could see those principles in His Word, then the next morning you go back to work, and when you get paid, you give and save as in the past because you have seen that is what God expects us to do. That is how He set life up. With this attitude there is no devastation if we lose it all."

There is a man in the Bible that lost it all—IN ONE DAY—including his children! –Job.

Job 1:22 In all this Job sinned not, nor charged God foolishly.

Job's main concern was his relationship with God. When God told Job—a man who had lost all children, all his wealth, and was covered in boils—to pray for his friends, he did exactly that. Here is a man who had God first in his heart.

When Job's troubles were over, God doubled back to him all his wealth. Interesting. I doubt that he opened the front door the next morning, and it was all sitting on his front step. Friends gave him some, but he must have known the principles of prosperity and simply put them back to work.

If you lose it all—if God is first in your life and your trust is in Him, you take it to Him in prayer.

When you pray, you can ask God to give you wisdom, as we read in James. He never berates you for asking. You could ask Him for wisdom every day, for things in general and for specific things, such as how to deal with finances and how to keep Him first. Ask Him to show you if you get off track.

You could read and study His Word. Part of what we read earlier in 3 John 1:2 was prospering as your soul prospers. Read and apply His Word in all the areas of your life that you can.

You can also ask God to teach you, lead you, and guide you. Maybe you are an adult and it might seem a little late in life to ask God to teach, lead, and guide you. In the Old Testament, David asked for those things, and he was a king. You would think a king would not ask to be taught, to be lead, or to be guided, but he did. And David's son, Solomon, asked God for wisdom!!

Psalm 144:1 (*A Psalm* of David.) Blessed *be* the LORD my strength, which **teacheth** my hands to war, *and* my fingers to fight:

Psalm 143:8-10 Cause me to hear thy lovingkindness in the morning; for in thee do I **trust:** cause me to know the way wherein I should walk; for I lift up my soul unto thee. Deliver me, O LORD, from mine enemies: I flee unto thee to hide me. **Teach me** to do thy will; for thou *art* my God: thy spirit *is* good; **lead me** into the land of uprightness.

Psalm 31:3 For thou *art* my rock and my fortress; therefore for thy name's sake **lead me**, and **guide me**.

2 Chronicles 1:10-12 Give me now wisdom and knowledge, that I may go out and come in before this people: for who can judge this thy people, *that is so* great? And God said to Solomon, Because this was in thine heart, and thou hast not asked riches, wealth, or honour, nor the life of thine enemies, neither yet hast asked long life; but hast asked wisdom and knowledge for thyself, that thou mayest judge my people, over whom I have made thee king: **Wisdom and knowledge *is* granted unto thee; and I will give thee riches, and wealth**, and honour, such as none of the kings have had that *have been* before thee, neither shall there any after thee have the like.

David, the king of Israel, asked God to teach him, to lead him, and to guide him. Solomon, the wisest man to live up until the day of Jesus Christ, asked God for wisdom. We could do the same daily as we pray, and then expect that our Father would do that for us also.

You might think of God as your older and wiser business partner. God's Word says that He is at work within you. Learn to pray for your family's finances. Ask Him to protect what you have stored and saved in your savings and funding accounts. Remember what we read in Malachi:

> **Malachi 3:11** And I will rebuke the devourer for your sakes, and he shall not destroy the fruits of your ground; neither shall your vine cast her fruit before the time in the field, saith the LORD of hosts.

God used agricultural illustrations because the people were so connected to the earth. We may not be farmers, but the promise of protection of what He has blessed us with is the same. Expect to see His hand at work in your finances to cause them to increase as you grow and learn. Even Satan recognized God's hand of blessing upon Job's financial life.

> **Job 1:10** Hast not thou made an hedge about him, and about his house, and about all that he hath on every side? thou hast blessed the work of his hands, and his substance is increased in the land.

Below is a great prayer from a man asking God to bless him. We are blessed with all spiritual blessings. This prayer concerns the physical realm here on the earth.

> **1 Chronicles 4:10** And Jabez called on the God of Israel, saying, Oh that thou wouldest bless me indeed, and enlarge my coast, and that thine hand might be with me, and that thou wouldest keep *me* from evil, that it may not grieve me! And God granted him that which he requested.

Why is this prayer in the Bible? Those things were written for our learning. We could also pray prayers like this. Ask and expect God's hand to be with us in all our endeavors. We are not alone in this work.

When you look at your accounts and see that some are depleting because they are being used, like the emergency fund, ask God for help in replenishing it. Don't wait till the fund is empty. Pray before you reach the bottom of the barrel. Guard your increase!

Pray for your savings and funding accounts. Pray for your investments. God is like a partner. Ultimately, it is His stuff anyway.

> **Psalm 24:1 A Psalm of David.** The earth *is* the LORD'S, and the fulness thereof; the world, and they that dwell therein.

> **1 Chronicles 29:14-16** But who *am* I, and what *is* my people, that we should be able to offer so willingly after this sort? for all things *come* of thee, and of thine own have we given thee. For we *are* strangers before thee, and sojourners, as *were* all our fathers: our days on the earth *are* as a shadow, and *there is* none abiding. O LORD our God, all this store that we have prepared to build thee an house for thine holy name *cometh* of thine hand, and *is* all thine own.

These last verses are on the occasion of David's dedication of the things he was giving to store up for the building of the temple by Solomon. David recognized that we are just stewards of the things we have. It all comes from God, and it all belongs to Him.

While we are here, we simply get to steward those things God gives us, and part of stewardship is to see the things under our care prosper and grow in value, the same as Joseph did in Potiphar's house.

> **Genesis 39:3** And his master saw that the LORD *was* with him, and that the LORD made all that he did to prosper in his hand.

If God made all that Joseph did to prosper, He will do the same for you and me. We, as stewards, are not just caretakers, but we are to see it grow also.

People used to work from daylight or earlier, until dark. So when you get home from work, work a couple of hours on learning how to cause your savings to grow. Learn to trade or buy and sell something.

> **Matthew 25:16-18** Then he that had received the five talents went and traded with the same, and made *them* other five talents. And likewise he that *had received* two, he also gained other two. But he that had received one went and digged in the earth, and hid his lord's money.

People used to trade for a profit. Obviously it was known how to do that in the lands and times of the Bible. It is a lost art. So get some books and read up.

Here are a couple of suggestions:
> One Red Paperclip: How to Trade a Red Paperclip for a House
> Kyle MacDonald
> Horse Tradin   Ben K. Green

Some people take their savings and buy and sell houses, boats, campers, antique glass or anything you can think of. Some sell it to dealers, on EBay, or on Craigslist.

Use the money in savings to buy and then put it all back along with the profit, minus your giving. The verses above do not say they made one trade to double their money. But when the householder came back, they had doubled it. That is much better than the bank!

In every venture you start, pray and ask God to give you understanding and wisdom, and to teach you, and to lead you, and to guide you. This, done over a period of years, will have some great success, because you are not alone in this venture. God is at work within you. You know He wants you to prosper. Learn to expect to see His wisdom and His guidance in your life.

CHAPTER 13

It Is Easy To Do

Many things in life are easy to do, and just as easy not to do.

- Put your change in a jar.
- Keep a thankful journal that you write in each evening.
- Make a list of Godly attributes that you want to include in your life philosophy, and review it every day.
- Tape a verse about something you want to acquire in your life to your bathroom mirror, and repeat it emphatically to yourself each day.

Easy to do, just as easy not to do.

But the long term effects are staggering. Money is easy to see and count, but the long term effects are the same whether it is money or thoughts.

When a thought is brought to mind daily or several times a day, some call that compounding. You could also use a mental image, which some say is more effective. Compounding is where one thing is added in on top of another, on top of another, on top of another, or two things are added together to expand your understanding In the latter case you would have thoughts on the same subject, a verse maybe, repeated over and over for months or years. That is a form of compounding. In others words, one thought is added on top of the last, and then again and again. This could give you a great increase in understanding and in believing that verse was true for you.

Compounding with savings is the same. If you saved $35.00/wk you would be compounding your savings each week. $35.00 + $35.00 +$35.00. Compounding! $35.00/week is $1,820.00/year. In the beginning, whether it is words or money, it does not seem like much. You don't see much in the way of results immediately. Over time, the results of what you are doing become apparent.

Easy to do, just as easy not to do

One author called this <u>The Slight Edge</u>. It is the difference between the wise described in Proverbs and the unwise. It is slight, but down the road the results can be incredible.

For instance: If you went over your savings and funding accounts once a week to find holes or to fine tune your financial engine, that would be wise. It is like correcting your steering while driving a car. Small adjustments.

Easy to do, just as easy not to do

Life is not set up for gigantic changes from one day into the next. Life is not set up on one roll of the dice. Someone once said that the wealthy were winners at the roulette table of life. In other words, the wealthy had just been lucky. Sometimes that may be the case, but that is not the way God designed life. Chance and gambling are very difficult to duplicate. Once the money gained this way is gone, it is just gone. This wisdom of knowing how God set life up to be lived is far more profitable than winning the lottery, or winning at the roulette table, or getting a professional sports contract. You cannot easily duplicate those things, but **the wisdom gained by believing and doing what God says in His word is priceless and can be done over and over**.

Proverbs 3:13-15 Happy *is* the man *that* findeth wisdom, and the man *that* getteth understanding. For the merchandise of it *is* better than the merchandise of silver, and the gain thereof than fine gold. She *is* more precious than rubies: and all the things thou canst desire are not to be compared unto her.

In this way, if you lost all your money, you know the principles of prosperity, and you can do it over again. This is why wisdom is more precious that rubies. It is slower than winning at the roulette table but far more predictable. Remember the story of the tortoise and the hare: slow and methodical is always better. I think we have already read that those hasty to be wealthy are not wise.

> **Proverbs 21:5** The thoughts of the diligent *tend* only to plenteousness; but of every one *that is* hasty only to want.

> **Galatians 6:7-9** Be not deceived; God is not mocked: for whatsoever a man soweth, that shall he also reap. For he that soweth to his flesh shall of the flesh reap corruption; but he that soweth to the Spirit shall of the Spirit reap life everlasting. And let us not be weary in well doing: for in due season we shall reap, if we faint not.

In sowing, you plant what you would normally eat in order to reap a much greater harvest. This requires patience. Jesus sowed the Word in people's lives, and at the end of his life it appeared that he was not too successful. At his death all men left him, and Peter denied he knew Jesus. Yet a couple of months later, Peter stood up on the day of Pentecost and preached, and about 3000 people got born again. It takes a while for the seed to grow. The same is true with your finances. You will always reap more than you sow. This sowing is in the area of giving, and you also sow to your savings. If you **give** or **save** sparingly, you will also **reap** sparingly. This principle of sowing and reaping is true in many areas of life.

> **That is the danger in bitterness, but it is also the blessing of forgiveness.**

Doing wise things over a long, long period of time produces amazing results, whether in relationships, finance, business, or in your walk with God. The problem with most of us is that we "get tired" of the journey. Half way through this journey, it looks like nothing is happening, and we become discouraged, disillusioned, and give up. However, what compounding teaches us is that a tomorrow that is built on what we learned yesterday or saved yesterday can grow and become something amazing. This is why the "little things matter" so much, **IF we don't quit**. As you come to grasp this truth, you begin to realize that the best is NOT behind, but ahead in this life AND in the next.

In order to get big results we must do the little things. Things that are

Easy to do, just as easy not to do.

When it comes to compounding, think about this:
"Beware of little expenses; a small leak will sink a great ship." Ben Franklin

Another example of compounding is a flywheel. If you have ever messed with a flywheel, you know that it takes some effort to get it spinning. If you keep pushing on it, it would be the same amount of energy added in with each push -- compounding. Once it is spinning, it only takes a small amount of additional effort to keep it going, and it will run on its own for a long time.

The following is an example of starting with an insignificant amount of money, a penny, and doubling the amount you have every day for 30 days. If you will notice by day 15, half way thru the month, we only have $163.84. Not much progress. Notice what happens in the last 15 days, though. It ends at $5.3 million. This is what compounding is about. It seems so small in the beginning, but it continues to build over time. Remember, this is just an illustration, not a prediction of your finances!

Day 1: $.01
Day 2: $.02
Day 3: $.04
Day 4: $.08
Day 5: $.16
Day 6: $.32
Day 7: $.64
Day 8: $1.28
Day 9: $2.56
Day 10: $5.12
Day 11: $10.24
Day 12: $20.48
Day 13: $40.96
Day 14: $81.92
Day 15: $163.84
Day 16: $327.68
Day 17: $655.36
Day 18: $1,310.72
Day 19: $2,621.44
Day 20: $5,242.88
Day 21: $10,485.76
Day 22: $20,971.52
Day 23: $41,943.04
Day 24: $83,886.08
Day 25: $167,772.16
Day 26: $335,544.32
Day 27: $671,088.64
Day 28: $1,342,177.28
Day 29: $2,684,354.56
Day 30: $5,368,709.12

With many things in life, the choices seem like they don't matter that much. In the beginning, there seems to be no difference. They are just choices. The choice

- To save $35.00 or go out to eat

- To go to your first fellowship or stay home, like your buddy.(In the end one choice could lead to eternal life and one not!)
- To marry one person or another
- To have one job or another or be self-employed
- To forgive or to be bitter
- To go to another meeting where someone is teaching the Word of God.
- To read a certain book or not.

The meeting you miss or the book you pass on reading may hold the key to your better life. Better to miss a meal than miss a book or a teaching, because you just don't know what you will learn. In that book or meeting, you may hear or read that one thing that puts you over the top.

These are just choices, but down the road the results may be huge, compared to what seemed to be a small choice.

> **Romans 12:1-2** I beseech you therefore, brethren, by the mercies of God, that ye present your bodies a living sacrifice, holy, acceptable unto God, *which is* your reasonable service. And be not conformed to this world: but be ye transformed by the renewing of your mind, that ye may prove what *is* that good, and acceptable, and perfect, will of God.

As with finances, this renewing of your mind is a slow process, but as time travels on, it will become apparent what has been going on inside your head and heart. It is a daily process. Remember the expression "an apple a day"? You don't get the same effect if you eat seven apples on Saturday night! The greatest effect comes from compounding daily.

Easy to do, just as easy not to do.

Deuteronomy 11:18 Therefore shall ye lay up these my words in your heart and in your soul, and bind them for a sign upon your hand, that they may be as frontlets between your eyes.

Proverbs 6:21-23 Bind them continually upon thine heart, *and* tie them about thy neck. When thou goest, it shall lead thee; when thou sleepest, it shall keep thee; and *when* thou awakest, it shall talk with thee. For the commandment *is* a lamp; and the law *is* light; and reproofs of instruction *are* the way of life:

We can choose to burn into our brains the things from God's Word that will light our paths. Thus, they become part of our philosophy, a way to conduct your lives.

So take the instructions in God's Word on finances, and put them in your heart. They are great wisdom, and there are some great promises, too. Ask God to teach you what **you** need to know for **your** life in relation to these things. And remember, it's…

Easy to do, just as easy not to do.

CHAPTER 14

Additional Thoughts

There are four very nice promises about receiving when we give.

> **Malachi 3:10** .... if I will not open you the windows of heaven, and pour you out a blessing, that *there shall* not *be room* enough *to receive it.*

> **Galatians 6:7** Be not deceived; God is not mocked: for whatsoever a man soweth, that shall he also reap.

> **2 Corinthians 9:6** But this *I say,* He which soweth sparingly shall reap also sparingly; and he which soweth bountifully shall reap also bountifully.

> **Luke 6:38** Give, and it shall be given unto you; good measure, pressed down, and shaken together, and running over, shall men give into your bosom. For with the same measure that ye mete withal it shall be measured to you again.

These are four illustrations of the same truth: as you give, you receive back much more than you gave.

When we read about the windows of heaven being opened and blessings pouring out, I think sometimes we feel that if we give, God will immediately shower gold coins down upon our head. Not seeing this come to pass right away can cause some to feel that giving does not work. But when God uses the illustration of sowing, we know that it takes a while once the seed is sown for the harvest to take place.

There is a rule in life that says that things that are equal to the same thing are equal to each other. If A equals D, and B equals D and C equals D, then A is equal to B, which is equal to C.

Very few things in life happen instantly. Prosperity is growth over time like most of the rest of things in God's creation. Children take years to grow up. Crops take months to grow. Our prosperity is not in our paycheck. It is in what we do with part of the check.

According to Dave Ramsey, if you put $35.00 per week away in a savings account, and invested it in a good growth stock mutual fund at 15%, you could retire in 40 years with $890,000.00 to $1.5 million. This could be done on a federal minimum wage. A very nice growth process.

If you worked at federal minimum wage for 40 years and retired a millionaire, could you feel like God opened the windows of heaven?

Prosperity is built over time rather than being a cash machine whereby we give and God then gives us rent money. This is not to say He will not or could not do that, but we need to take a long term perspective on prosperity. It is not how much you make, but what you do with what you make. Do you spend it all or save part? It is a huge difference down the road.

So as you give and save remember to be patient. You don't reap the day after you sow. But it will come back to you, pressed down, shaken together and running over so that over time it will be like the windows of heaven are open to you.

Faithful in little

Luke 16:10-12 He that is faithful in that which is least is faithful also in much: and he that is unjust in the least is unjust also in much. If therefore ye have not been faithful in the unrighteous mammon, who will commit to your trust the true *riches?* And if ye have not been faithful in that which is another man's, who shall give you that which is your own?

What we give and/or save in the beginning may not seem to be much, but it is the faithfulness that is important. As we are faithful in the least or the little amounts, God will then be able to trust us with more. Notice, money is a carnal thing, the unrighteous mammon. The true riches would be a greater understanding of God's Word. **If you want more understanding of the Word, become faithful or even more faithful in the physical or carnal things and in carrying out that which God asks us to do.**

The rich getting rich on the backs of the poor

Matthew 13:12 For whosoever hath, to him shall be given, and he shall have more abundance: but whosoever hath not, from him shall be taken away even that he hath.

This verse is spoken in the context of understanding, but it is also true in the area of finance. If you are faithful to give and save, you will receive even more, but if you spend all you bring in, eventually, that tends to poverty. This is why the rich many times get richer. It is because they understand the foundational principles of prosperity and practice them, on the other hand the poor either are ignorant of the principles or just don't care and become poorer.

Proverbs 11:24-25 There is that scattereth, and yet increaseth; and *there is* that withholdeth more than is meet, but *it tendeth* to poverty. The liberal soul shall be made fat: and he that watereth shall be watered also himself.

Prosperity of Christians and Non-Christians

During one of the recessions we had in Oklahoma, the oil prices collapsed to around $10.00/barrel. I had a friend who did accounting who me that one of the things she observed in keeping books for some of the small companies in Oklahoma was that the companies that weathered the recession well were companies that were givers. Christian or non-Christian, it did not seem to matter. These companies gave out of their income every month. The companies that did not do well were the companies that did not give at all, and it made no difference whether they were Christian or non-Christian.

If the poor practiced the principles of giving and saving, eventually, they would no longer be the poor.

The Poverty Mentality

Money does not change you, it just magnifies who you are. If your habit is to spend all you make, then if you win the lottery, or receive a large pro sports contract, you will just continue as in the past. You just have more to spend. This is truly a poverty mentality.

It is the fundamentals that keep you prosperous. A lack of knowledge of the fundamentals keeps you broke. For instance, professional athletes make a lot of money, but many never instilled in their lives what to do with it, and thus many of them go broke.

Spending as a Part of Prosperity

> **2 Chronicles 1:15a** And the king (Solomon) made silver and gold at Jerusalem *as plenteous* as stones,

Remember, Solomon was the wisest man that lived until Jesus Christ. With that wisdom, he spent part of the great wealth that God gave him. In spending it, he scattered it throughout the people of Jerusalem to the end that God said that silver and gold were as plenteous as stones in Jerusalem.

Money in the Gospels

Jesus Christ many times used physical things such as money to teach spiritual truths. Some say money comes up in just under 50% of the parables in the gospels. It might be interesting to go through the gospels and make a note about how many times Jesus Christ spoke about money or used money as part of an illustration in a parable.

It is not what you get that is important; it is what you become in the process.

CHAPTER 15

What to Do if You Are over 60

I was talking to friend of mine a month ago or so, and he said, "I get it with what you are saying. I can see how these young people can really do this stuff, but what am I to do? I am over 60; I can't save enough to retire on."

In the Old Testament there is a record of three men who were told to bow to a statue made of gold set up in the plains of Dura. If they did not bow, they would burn in a fiery furnace. They had a fellow servant of God, Daniel, who had been told by the king's law that the only prayers to be offered for the next 30 days were to be offered to the king and any that refused would be thrown into a den of hungry lions. You can read all through the Old Testament up to that point, and there are not any promises of deliverance from a burning fiery furnace, and no promise of deliverance from a den of hungry lions. What were these men to do? God's Word shows us the nature of God, what He is like. Through the records that were available to those men and from what they had heard of God, they knew of God's love, His compassion, His care, His protection in battle, His mercy, His great power, and His promises of protection for those who love Him. God is the same yesterday, today, and forever. If he had mercy on others, he will have mercy on you. These men trusted that as God had delivered others in dire straits in the past, that He would deliver them also. And He did. The men were thrown into the burning fiery furnace, and God sent His angel to protect them. They walked out alive with not even the smell of smoke on them.

Similarly, God sent his angel to shut the lion's mouths for Daniel, and Daniel had not a scratch.

We are going to read a parable that also shows the nature of God in another situation.

> **Matthew 20:1-16** For the kingdom of heaven is like unto a man *that is* an householder, which went out early in the morning to hire labourers into his vineyard. And when he had agreed with the labourers for a penny a day, he sent them into his vineyard. And he went out about the third hour, and saw others standing idle in the marketplace, And said unto them; Go ye also into the vineyard, and whatsoever is right I will give you. And they went their way. Again he went out about the sixth and ninth hour, and did likewise. And about the eleventh hour he went out, and found others standing idle, and saith unto them, Why stand ye here all the day idle? They say unto him, Because no man hath hired us. He saith unto them, Go ye also into the vineyard; and whatsoever is right, *that* shall ye receive. So when even was come, the lord of the vineyard saith unto his steward, Call the labourers, and give them *their* hire, beginning from the last unto the first. And when they came that *were hired* about the eleventh hour, they received every man a penny. But when the first came, they supposed that they should have received more; and they likewise received every man a penny. And when they had received *it,* they murmured against the goodman of the house, Saying, These last have wrought *but* one hour, and thou hast made them equal unto us, which have borne the burden and heat of the day.
>
> But he answered one of them, and said, Friend, I do thee no wrong: didst not thou agree with me for a penny? Take *that* thine *is,* and go thy way: I will give unto this last, even as unto thee. Is it not lawful for me to do what I will with mine own? Is thine eye evil, because I am good? So the last shall be first, and the first last: for many be called, but few chosen.

Many of us learned about saving money from God's Word pretty late in life. If, in the parable, the householder paid the last the same as the first, I would trust that God would not hold it against us that we came so late to the party. His promises of prosperity are true at any age. They have no expiration dates. God will not look at you and say, "Too late, you should have started earlier in the day."

No, His promises are true at any age. God is full of mercy, love and compassion, and His promises fail not. Just get busy. Set up your bank accounts and pray. Remember when you pray, not to beg. Children don't beg from their fathers. Children ask expecting their fathers to do as the father has promised. Likewise, we too should pray with great expectation that our Heavenly Father will do as He has promised. Many of the prayers in the Bible are of men praying back to God with God's own words. Like this: "Father you have promised in your Word that you will supply all our needs, and we have a need. I need a retirement for my wife, and I am thankful that You have promised to meet our needs. I just rest my life on your Words and expect to see Your Word come to pass as I carry out what You have said." Something like that.

Then learn to trade with the money in the accounts. Find a means to make it grow and trade with it. Start small and grow to bigger things if you want. Have fun. You have an advantage being older in that you have seen a lot more, been exposed to a lot more, so that you mentally have more to draw on in finding something in which to trade.

> **Matthew 25:16-17** Then he that had received the five talents went and traded with the same, and made *them* other five talents. And likewise he that *had received* two, he also gained other two.

These men did not just put the money in the bank. They went and doubled their money over time. You can do the same. Just because trading is a lost art does not mean we can't learn it. I gave you a list earlier of money doubled and how rapidly it grows and multiplies. Use your age and wisdom and your relationship with your Father to have some new adventures in trading and seeing His promises come to pass.

I told you about the book of the man that in 14 trades traded a paperclip for a house. Learn how to trade, do it with your Father, and have a great time.

Conclusion

In conclusion, I wanted to leave you with some thoughts on the profit of doing what God has said:

> **Psalm 119:98-100** Thou through thy commandments hast made me wiser than mine enemies: for they [His commandments] *are* ever with me. I have more understanding than all my teachers: for thy testimonies *are* my meditation. I understand more than the ancients, because I keep thy precepts.

As you understand some of the things we have covered, put them into action in your life, and if you expect God to teach you, He will open your eyes to even more. The Psalmist said he understood more than the ancients because he kept God's Word. Great understanding of God's Word can be yours also as you meditate on it and do it.

As we close, remember where we started. God's will for your life is this:

> **3 John 1:2 Beloved, I wish above all things that thou mayest prosper and be in health, even as thy soul prospereth.**

Now, put God's Word in your heart, pray a lot, be a giver, a saver, and a trader, and eventually, we will meet when the Lord returns at the sound of the trumpet.

> We will be surprised at the bema how many rewards are given for stewardship in the physical realm.
> Lifelines, VPW

List of Additional Resources

The Financial Peace Planner
A Step-by-Step Guide to Restoring Your Family's Financial Health
By Dave Ramsey
ISBN-13: 978-0140264685
ISBN-10: 014026468X

Rich Dad's CASHFLOW Quadrant
Rich Dad's Guide to Financial Freedom
ISBN-10: 1612680054
ISBN-13: 978-1612680057

The Traveler's Gift
Seven Decisions that Determine Personal Success
ISBN-10: 0785273220
ISBN-13: 978-0785273226

The Richest Man in Babylon
Six Laws of Wealth
ISBN-10: 1490348557
ISBN-13: 978-1490348551

Challenge to Succeed 4 Disc Set
by Jim Rohn

The Storehouse principle
A Revolutionary God Idea For Creating Extraordinary Financial Stability
By Crouch Van
ISBN-10: 1593790554
ISBN-13: 978-1593790554

Healing from God is Available
By Michael A. Verdicchio
ISBN-10: 1449954332
ISBN-13: 978-1449954338

Made in the USA
Coppell, TX
25 April 2024

31720450R00069